A HISTORICAL PERSPECTIVE

*St. Bartley Primitive Baptist Church v.
The United States Government`*

REV. DR. ISAIAH ROBINSON JR.

WESTBOW
PRESS®
A DIVISION OF THOMAS NELSON
& ZONDERVAN

WestBow Press books may be ordered through booksellers or by contacting:

WestBow Press
A Division of Thomas Nelson & Zondervan
1663 Liberty Drive
Bloomington, IN 47403
www.westbowpress.com
844-714-3454

Interior Image Credit: Rev. Dr. Isaiah Robinson Jr.

ISBN: 978-1-6642-2893-1 (sc)
ISBN: 978-1-6642-2894-8 (hc)
ISBN: 978-1-6642-2892-4 (e)

Library of Congress Control Number: 2021906294

Print information available on the last page.

WestBow Press rev. date: 09/08/2021

CONTENTS

Acknowledgments vii

Preface xi

Chapter 1   Introduction to St. Bartley Primitive Baptist Church 1

Chapter 2   Historical Aspects of Madison County, Alabama 8

Chapter 3   How It All Began for the African Baptist Church
in Huntsville, Alabama 17

Chapter 4   The Beginning of a New Era 36

Chapter 5   The People and Events of the New Era 55

Chapter 6   The Census Data of 1860, 1870, 1880, and 1900 69

Chapter 7   The Court of Claims of the United States, 1901–1906.... 71

Chapter 8   St. Bartley Primitive Baptist Church - 1900–Present 78

Reflections 95

Summary of Claims against the US Government 99

Final Summary and Reflections 101

References and Resources 109

Exhibits 115

ACKNOWLEDGMENTS

First of all, I am eternally grateful to God for His grace and His mercy toward me. If it had not been for the Lord on my side, I don't know where I would be now. I am who I am because of the calling God placed on my life to preach His Word. There is no greater love than the love I have for God, who has been with me through the fire and through the flood as He promised. This research and works are the result of the guidance of the Holy Spirit and the empowerment of His actions upon the slaves at that time that has allow the truth to be told of this great church and this great people of God.

This book is dedicated to my wife, Viola D. Robinson; my sons, Chris, Chauncey, Cameron, and Chad; my daughters, Aurelia and Donna; my father, the Rev. Isaiah Robinson Sr. (deceased); my mother, Aneva Robinson (deceased); my parental grandparents, Deacon John and Thula Robinson (deceased); and my maternal grandmother, Mother Daisy Cullins (deceased). To Elder W. L. Braggs (deceased), from whom I first learned the doctrine and ways of the Primitive Baptist, and my grandparents. To Elder Amos Robinson (deceased), Elder T. M. Batts (deceased), Elder G. W. Gibson (deceased), Elder F. L. Livingston (deceased), and Elder F. W. Blackwell (deceased), all of whom mentored and tutored me in the doctrine of the church and the preaching of the totality of the Gospel of Jesus Christ.

I can never say thank you enough to my brother-in-law, the Reverend Dr. Wylheme Ragland, retired pastor in the United Methodist Church and a great historian who challenged me to research and write this material. This journey started in June 2014. It entailed much research; long nights and early mornings talking with God; and a review of various sources and research into various documents. Along it, I felt the presence of the slaves, who were determined to become closer to God, and prayed to God for guidance so

He would get all the glory and honor for the mighty works He'd done for the first black church in Alabama started by slaves. I owe Dr. Ragland so much for his assistance and guidance.

After attending Garrett Theological Seminary on the campus of Northwestern University in Evanston, Illinois, I became keenly inquisitive about the black church and its impact upon the world. Elder Amos Robinson wanted me to write a curriculum for the Saint Bartley Primitive Baptist Church so that an effective Christian education program could be instituted and the congregation would have more biblical knowledge of God and His plan and His Will for humankind. The ideal was to glorify God and edify humanity on the wonderful God we serve—to give a biblical foundation yet make it relevant for the present day. During the existence of the Primitive Baptist Church, much emphasis was on preaching, praying, and singing; very little was on the teaching aspects as directed by Jesus and recorded in Matthew 28:18–20.

After forty years of pastoring at the Pilgrim Rest Primitive Baptist Church in the Birmingham, Alabama, community and four years pastoring at the Morning Star Missionary Baptist Church in Stevenson, Alabama, and interim pastoring at St. Bartley Church for three years, I'm indebted to the members of those churches for their love and devotion; they challenged me week by week to keep preaching the liberating Gospel of Jesus Christ and the Holy Word of God. Among them were my sister, Shirley Robinson Tolliver, and brother, Leon Robinson.

I can never say thank you enough to those with whom I've had the pleasure to join in labor on this Gospel journey. There are numerous preachers, pastors, teachers, and lay leaders who have been my mentors and my spiritual eyes and ears and provided me with the protected spirituality I've needed to do God's will.

I am indebted to many for my present level of intellectual and spiritual growth. Among those are the Rev. Dr. Jasper Williams Jr., Rev. Dr. T. L. Lewis, Elder Amos Robinson, Elder V. Castle Stewart, Rev. Dr. Julius R. Scruggs, Elder Ezell Tibbs, Elder T. M. Batts, Elder Dr. F. L. Livingston, Elder B. A. Hemphill, Rev. Dr. H. P. Snodgrass, Rev. Dr. Gordon

Humphrey Sr., Rev. L. F. Lacy, Rev. Robert Richards, Rev. N. H. Smith, Deacon John W. Laughinghouse Sr., Deacon John W. Laughinghouse Jr., Deacon D. G. Robinson, Mother Josephine Robinson, Mother Effie Gaines, Sister Eunice Betts Scott, Rev. Richard Johnson, Rev. W. L. Mayes, Rev. J. C. Coleman, Bishop Jasper Roby, Professor T. E. Weatherly, Deacon A. L. Morris, Mr. Moses Brewer, Rev. Leroy and Mother Jackie Sawyer, Mr. Charlie Johnson Jr., Mr. Herbert "Sonny" Evans, Mr. Allen Ben Cothron, Mr. Nathaniel Stearns, Mr. Walter Lee Clay, Mr. John Eddie Henry, Deacon John and Mother Doris Hutchins, Rev. Jesse Jackson, Rev. Clay Evans, and many, many more who have been patient with me and have been shoulders to lean on, especially during my weakest hour. To each of them. I extend my love. There are many, many others, too numerous to name. Much wisdom was obtained from my mother-in-law, Mrs. Viola Ragland, and my father-in-law, Mr. Howard Ragland. My grandmother Thula Robinson taught me to sing the Dr. Watts hymns of the church. Many times, as she and other mothers of the church prepared items for Communion, they would pray, sing hymns, and shout as flour and other items would go flying through the air.

The guidance of God through this journey has been marvelous. Many moments, the Holy Spirit has spoken to me and guided me to bring out the many aspects of how this great church, the St. Bartley Primitive Baptist church, which started in a graveyard, and the impact it had upon the people at that time. Many nights and early mornings while writing, I could feel the presence of the Holy Spirit and the spirit of the slaves and how they praised God for his wonderful works, even in their singing of freedom songs such as "Wade in the Water, Children"; "Sit Down, Servant"; "Swing Low Sweet Chariot"; "There's a Great Meeting in the Old Campground"; "Father, I Stretch My Hands to Thee"; "Amazing Grace"; and many other that kept their spirits upheld.

There were times I felt as if they were assisting me in writing this material. I could sense the leadership and powerful preaching of Elder Bartley Harris; the courage and fearlessness of the founder, Elder William Harris; the pastoral abilities of the other ministers; and the powerful preaching and moaning of Elder Richard Moore and Elder Amos Robinson. There too were the joy of Deacon John W. Laughinghouse, Sr., as well as the happiness of "Button and John Wesley," both great friends and inspiration to me who kept me moving forward. There were times I cried because of the impact of the Holy Spirit as He gave direction and utterance of this work. The research and writing of this book have been a blessing and an inspiration, giving way to a deeper appreciation of the steadfast love those slaves had for the church. The church was so important to them that it meant spiritual uplifting and hope for freedom.

The slaves who worshipped in the Georgia Graveyard were dedicated totally to God. Their goals were for freedom, spiritual uplifting, hope, and total trust in God and to give God all honor and glory. Even though they were contained, their spirits, through togetherness, were united in one strong band of Christian love for each other and for each of them to succeed. They believed that freedom would come only through God.

During the latter part of 1866 and on after the Civil War, many blacks occupied political offices, and outstanding leadership was provided to the community. The men dressed to impress and were always fashionable but dedicated to the task.

During the formation of the National Primitive Baptist Convention in 1906 in Huntsville, Alabama, the elders were well educated in the Spirit of the Lord and in the Word of God. They had great inspiration, courage, and faith and established many schools of learning in churches and in various communities throughout Alabama, Florida, and other areas. These were great leaders of the church, and the church was the center of the community and the foundation of the black community. Men were called and ordained by God to do a specific work for the kingdom, and they did so with zeal, love, and great determination to please God. May God forever be given the glory, honor, and praise.

PREFACE

I am convinced that the black church needs to heighten its awareness of and strengthen its emphasis on the meaning of faith and hope in the daily lives of Christians.

Symbolically, the black church has always represented more than a house of worship. Metaphorically, it has represented the protector of black bodies; the educator of black girls and boys; and the audacious voice that believes, even now and against all evidence to the contrary, that African American lives not only matter but are also capable of redeeming the soul of an unrepentantly racist nation.

Slaves shaped the tenets of Christianity to help them survive and preserve their bodies and souls. Slaves expressed their hope of freedom inside and outside church walls. They sang of freedom in the fields, preached it to their brethren in the slave quarters, and shouted it in churches and chapels. They combined the Christian celebration of the individual soul with an African indifference to the self-mutilating qualities of sin and repentance to fashion a powerful uplifting force that helped facilitate personal and community survival.

They also expressed their hopes in spirituals, songs that became outpourings of sorrow and hope. The songs showed the daily experiences of slaves as they toiled on Earth and hoped for solace from heaven. They sang of freedom, the future new order, and the justice of Christ's last judgment. These are some of the things Elder William Harris taught the slaves in the Georgia Graveyard as they yearned for freedom and yet was guided by a greater desire for God.

During brush arbor services in the Georgia Graveyard, slaves sung both hymnbook songs and their own vocal expressions of life experiences and trials. They emphasized the importance of prayer in the services, and brush arbor prayers could be long and intense as both those who prayed and those who listened experienced the emotions present in their petitions. The services entered a trance-like level of emotion when the participants began the ring out and shout. Shouts normally began with the service leader proclaiming a promise from the Bible. The participants would respond by shuffling in circles around the leader and shouting their affirmation. They would continue the process long into the night, placing themselves in trances and opening the path to direct communication with the spiritual world.

The brush arbor meeting in the Georgia Graveyard was important to slaves in many respects. As blacks gathered to worship, they could express their desires in ways they could not do on the plantation, save for the messages encoded in spirituals. They had the opportunity to celebrate themselves and their unique heritage through the actions and rituals of the meetings, and they cultivated a modicum of self-esteem from those meetings that worried whites.

The black church in the United States can be traced back to in the United States back to chattel slavery in the eighteenth and nineteenth centuries. Enslaved Africans brought to the Americas a variety of religions, including traditional spiritual practices. But the system of slavery was built on the dehumanization and exploitation of enslaved people, and this could only be achieved by depriving slaves of meaningful connections to land, ancestry, and identity. The dominant white culture of the time accomplished this through a system of forced acculturation, which included forced religious conversion.

During the decades of slavery in America, slave associations were a constant source of concern to slave owners. For many members of white society, black religious meetings symbolized the ultimate threat to white existence. Nevertheless, African slaves established and relied heavily on their churches. Religion offered a means of catharsis. Africans retained their faith in God and found refuge in their churches. However, white society was not always willing to accept the involvement of slaves in Christianity. As one slave recounted, "The white folks would come in when the colored people would have prayer meeting and whip every one of them.

---

[1] Charles O. Boothe, Charles O. *The Cyclopedia of the Colored Baptists of Alabama* (1895), 7.

Most of them thought that when colored people were praying it was against them."

Religious exercises of slaves were closely watched to detect plans for escape or insurrection. African American churches showed an air of militancy in the eyes of white Americans. Insurrections such as Nat Turner's in Virginia, born out of the religious inspiration of slaves, horrified white Americans. Understanding the potential end that could result from the religious experiences of African slaves, many white Americans opposed the participation of blacks in Christianity. In African American history, "the church" has long been at the center of black communities. It has established itself as the greatest source of African American religious enrichment and secular development.

The origin of the black church in the Georgia Graveyard founded by William Harris was more important in the lives of its congregation and the community as compared to that of other churches.. This was the first black church in Huntsville and in Alabama, the First African Baptist Church, which later became known as the Saint Bartley Primitive Baptist Church.

The services in the Georgia Graveyard were very spiritual. They usually involved a devotional prayer provided by a leading member of the church, singing by the congregation, and the minister's sermon. The prayer would request a powerful God to ease the earthly burden of the congregation and would be enhanced by the congregation's response, an expression of agreement with the words, "Yes, Lord," "Have mercy, Lord," and "Amen."

After the prayer, the congregation typically showed its devotion through song. Occasionally an individual member would stand up and lead the house in song.

The third element in a classic black service was the minister's sermon. Building on the long tradition of slave preachers and "exhorters," many ministers employed all the drama and poetry at their command, injecting vivid imagery and analogy into their biblical accounts, conveying understanding of the rewards of righteousness and the wages of sin. For these people, the black church was indeed "a rock in a weary land."

The Georgia Graveyard gave birth to the Saint Bartley Primitive Baptist Church and birth to a new atmosphere of praises unto God. It is my desire that you, the readers of these words, will find in them some measure of joy, inspiration, challenge, and appreciation toward a deeper, more satisfying faith in God and a nobler light of hope for every dark experience that may confront you, knowing that the slaves overcame such hardships and trials by their faith in God. If they did so, then we too can do the same. Thank God for Saint Bartley Primitive Baptist Church. This historical perspective of Saint Bartley Primitive Baptist Church is written to give God all the Glory, honor, and praise. He is worthy to be praised and glorified. It is His marvelous work upon this church and these His people that has become a living testimony of the awesomeness of God. To God be the Glory for the great things He has done.

This work is a compilation of over six years of research and gathering of materials that would enhance the true meaning of church and what the church is all about. All honor, glory, and praise are given to God though the Holy Spirit that led me and guided me in writing this book. This book is written to the glory of God and to honor and praise His Holy Name.

INTRODUCTION TO ST. BARTLEY PRIMITIVE BAPTIST CHURCH

As a youth growing up in Scottsboro, Alabama, I was introduced to the Primitive Baptist Church by my parental grandparents, John and Thula Robinson, of Hollywood, Alabama. It was through them that I learned the Dr. Watts's hymns and the techniques, as well as the principles and practices of the Primitive Baptist faith. Later, Elder Will Bragg, who pastored the Shiloh Primitive Baptist Church in Hollywood, Alabama, founded the White Rock Primitive Baptist Church in Stevenson, Alabama, along with my grandparents and Deacon Homer Rutledge and his wife. That was the extent of my knowledge of the Primitive Baptist Church in that area. However, while traveling with Elder Bragg and my grandparents, I was able to visit various Primitive Baptist associations, such as Lynn Creek: Flint River and Running Water: Ironsides, Cumberland: and Big Harpeth. It was a learning experience along the way. Rev. Bragg used to sit me on a stool in the pulpit near him at Shiloh and White Rock. These services were long—all day—and tedious.

Growing up in Scottsboro, I was connected with the St. Elizabeth Missionary Baptist Church. I was baptized at the age of twelve, along with my sister, Shirley, who was ten, on the first Saturday in May 1957, in an outlet of the Tennessee River by the Rev. M. C. Harris, pastor of St. Elizabeth Missionary Baptist Church. and I was fellowshipped into the church on the first Sunday in May 1957. It was through the experiences of Sunday school, BTU, and other ministries of the church we learned to grow spiritually. I was called into the ministry by God at the age of twelve and didn't know how to respond. I asked the Lord to allow me to become a stronger Christian before I began. The Lord allowed it.

Our family lived in Chattanooga, Tennessee, for a while, and there we united with the Olivet Baptist Church under the pastorate of Rev. Robert Richards. After a period in Chattanooga, our family moved back to Scottsboro and back to St. Elizabeth. While in Chattanooga, I attended Westside Elementary School; Second District Junior High; and, for a short time, Howard High School. I learned the streets and the things that went on in the streets. I joined a gang and, eventually, the Blackstone Rangers. I hustled numbers for the number men and made a small amount of money to assist my family. With the indoctrination of the church and other teachings, I learned much of the work of the church and the importance of salvation.

We were back and forth from Scottsboro to Chattanooga. Once permanently back in Scottsboro, I attended G. W. Carver High School. I started in elementary school at the age of four and a half because my birth certificate was changed to reflect six years of age. My first-grade teacher was Ms. Imogene Snodgrass. She was the sister of the Rev. Horace Perkins Snodgrass. She, Rev. Snodgrass, and my father were close friends and had gone to elementary school together in Hollywood. Ms. Snodgrass was a favorite of mine, and I was a favorite of hers. She treated me like I was her child and taught me so much that I was well advanced in scholarly learning by age six. My father, who went to the eighth grade in school, along with Ms. Snodgrass, taught me how to read and write. My father was very good in math; it was just a gift he had. After the first grade, I was skipped to the third grade and then to the fifth grade. In Chattanooga, I started at Westside Fifth Street Elementary School in the fifth grade, attended Second District Junior High, and eventually attended Howard High School.

I learned valuable lessons from guys I met and associated with, such as Noah Nelson, Raymond Stargin, Alvin Styles, and Leroy McComb. At the age of fifteen, I graduated from G. W. Carver High School as valedictorian in May 1964. In the church, I continued to work, study and apply myself to the teachings of Christ. At the age of seventeen, I accepted my call to the ministry after God had again given me the opportunity to work for the kingdom of God. My calling took place while I was a student at Tennessee A & I University in Nashville.

The first Sunday in May 1965, I preached my initial sermon at St. Elizabeth Missionary Baptist Church, and I was ordained along with my father, Isaiah Sr., at the Mud Creek Missionary Baptist Association in September 1965 by the Rev. Dr. H. P. Snodgrass (the moderator and pastor of First Baptist Church in Huntsville) and a host of other ministers who made up the presbytery. The event took place at the association that was held at the Old Farmer's Capital building in Madison County, Alabama.

In 1964/65, I attended Tennessee A& I University in Nashville. I was on a scholarship. In 1966, due to my mother's health, I transferred from Tennessee State University and enrolled in Alabama A&M University. I joined the First Missionary Baptist Church in Huntsville, Alabama, while in college there. Dr. H. P. Snodgrass was pastor. Dr. Snodgrass and my father were childhood friends. Both attended school and lived as youths in Hollywood. He readily accepted me and began to teach me many aspects of the church and of preaching. He emphasized the importance of studying God's Word and the utilization of biblical resources. Through him and the Rev. Richard Johnson, who was now pastor of St. Elizabeth, I was offered the opportunity to travel and attend with them various national Baptist conventions and congresses.

Having to study under Dr. Snodgrass, I was constantly inquiring about the aspects of learning more about the work of the church, pastoring, and all ministries.

In May 1968, I married my college sweetheart, Viola Doris Ragland, of Anniston, Alabama. We both attended First Missionary Baptist Church. While living in Scottsboro, we attended St. Elizabeth Missionary Baptist Church. Upon leaving Scottsboro and moving to Huntsville joined the First Missionary Baptist Church in Huntsville.

On one occasion while in attendance at the Huntsville Interdenominational Ministerial Alliance, which was held monthly at First Missionary Baptist Church, I met the Rev. Amos Robinson. I found Rev. Amos Robinson to be an outstanding minister, pastor, and person. He had a humble spirit and was a great example of what a minister should be. He was constantly witnessing to people about Christ everywhere he went. Rev. Amos Robinson was the pastor of St. Bartley Primitive Baptist Church in Huntsville.

On several occasions, Rev. Snodgrass allowed me to preach on the third Sundays because this was usually the Sunday set aside for the youth of the church. On one occasion while at Alabama A&M, I met Francina Mitchell, who was a member of St. Bartley Primitive Baptist Church. She invited me to come and speak on their annual youth day program. Rev. Robinson consented, and I went to St. Bartley.

As I preached, I emphasized some of the doctrines of the Primitive Baptist Church and how important they were for members to learn and instill in their lives, as well as the abstracts and principles of the Word of God. The chairman of the deacon board of St. Bartley, Deacon John W. Laughinghouse Sr., could not believe I was so profound in the doctrine

4

at such a young age and challenged me as to how I knew those aspects. I informed him of my background and the teachings I'd received from Elder Will Bragg, Elder F. T. Blackwell, and my grandparents.

Later, at one of the ministerial alliance meetings, Rev. Amos Robinson asked if I would come to St. Bartley and serve as his assistant in developing a Christian education program at the church and with the Indian Creek Primitive Baptist Association. I told him I would have to pray over it and get Rev. Snodgrass's permission. My professional occupation was teaching math at Chapman Middle School. I was up each morning around 5:30 a.m.with phone calls from Rev. Robinson and Deacon Laughinghouse, Sr. They never missed a day or time.

Finally, after Rev. Robinson and Rev. Snodgrass got together, Rev. Snodgrass informed Rev. Robinson he would loan me to him for a period of time, but I was still his member. From that moment on, I became involved with the St. Bartley Primitive Baptist Church.

Rev. Robinson was delighted for me to come to St. Bartley. It was at St. Bartley that my children were blessed by the Rev. B. A. Hemphill. I worked diligently with Rev. Robinson. I traveled with him on weekend days to various members' homes and hospitals to visit the sick and attended meetings and so forth, driving him while he talked and nodded. We developed a great friendship and fellowship.

Rev. Robinson, a great visionary, became a great mentor and just like a father to me. He demonstrated great love for me, and I likewise for him. I learned the many facets and the history of the church and some of the trials it had to endure. I learned the full impact and love that a pastor must have for his members. Rev. Robinson loved all his members, and the spiritual touch he had with them was remarkable. He truly loved me and shared many things of his life and the ministry with me.

Rev. Robinson was in the process of doing something that the Primitive Baptist did not do at that time, and that was to make me his assistant pastor. All ministers who belonged to a Primitive Baptist Church at that time were considered associate ministers, who basically carried out instructions given by the pastor, such as reading the scripture on Sunday and conducting offertory prayer. This was a new adventure. He was a progressive and spiritually minded pastor. However, before the next church conference in which he was going to obtain church approval for the position, the Lord called him home. He went to be with the Lord on the second Sunday in May 1970.

From the period of Rev. Amos Robinson's death, the church asked me to serve as interim pastor until a new pastor was elected. I had many ideas of the continued growth and progress of the church, much of which I'd learned from Rev. Amos Robinson. The members inquired of me about accepting the position as pastor. However, many of them thought I was too young to be in that position and wanted an older and more experienced person.

In 1970, I attended the National Primitive Baptist Convention, USA, Inc. in Austin, Texas. Elder Eugene Lewis was sent as the official delegate of the church. In 1971, the church sent me as a delegate to Cleveland, Ohio, to the National Primitive Baptist Convention, USA, Inc. as its official delegate. It was my first Primitive Baptist Convention. . Elder T.M. Batts, who became a friend and mentor to me, along with Elder G. W. Gibson, introduced me to many of the elders. Among those were Elder P. D. Brantley, Elder F. L. Livingston, Elder B. A. Hemphill, Elder M. D. Miles, and many others. Elder B.A. Hemphill and I became close friends and he served as my mentor. They were impressed with me for being the youngest elder to ever attend the convention and for my knowledge of the Primitive Baptist faith. I continued to serve as interim pastor until October 1972, when Elder V. Castle Stewart became the seventh pastor of St. Bartley.

I served under the leadership of Elder Stewart. In September 1973, Elder Stewart's connection with Dr. Carl Marbury, an instructor at Garrett Theological Seminary in Evanston, Illinois, on the campus of Northwestern University, was able to obtain me a full scholarship to attend the seminary there. So, with my faith in God, I left to study and become more aware of the goodness of God, as well as His grace and mercy. When entering Garrett, I felt a degree of fear of, not knowing what to expect. I was sure of my calling into the ministry by God. And being the only Primitive Baptist there, I was somewhat apprehensive about what to expect. With my undergraduate and graduate degrees that I obtained from Alabama A&M University I was able to complete the M. Div. Degree in August 1975.

Upon returning to St. Bartley, I was given the opportunity to work with Elder Stewart and the Indian Creek Primitive Baptist Association, Inc. and the National Primitive Baptist Convention, USA, Inc. I was called to pastor the Pilgrim Rest Primitive Baptist Church in Brighton, Alabama (a suburb of Birmingham, Alabama), and I served there for a total of forty years.

After I retired as pastor, the church voted to give me the title of Pastor Emeritus. Later, I served four years at the Morning Star Missionary Baptist Church in Stevenson, Alabama, for four years. Afterward, I returned to my home church, First Missionary Baptist Church, under the pastorship of Dr. Julius R. Scruggs. Dr. Scruggs was a great mentor to me as well as a close friend. With my ministry I was still eager to learn and to apply more toward church growth, church administration, leadership, financial management, Christian Education and pastoral care. Rev. Dr. Jasper Williams, Jr. was instrumental in serving as a trainer and mentor to me in this spiritual growth. Everyone thought we were brothers due to some similarities. The fellowship and relationship established with Dr. Williams was very inspiring and spiritually rewarding. Rev. Dr. Tommie L. Lewis, Pastor of Bethel Baptist Church in Pratt City,, Alabama proved to be a very close friend as well and was just like a brother to me.

HISTORICAL ASPECTS OF
MADISON COUNTY, ALABAMA

In 1808, Madison County was created by the governor of the Mississippi territory, who named it after President James Madison (1751–1836).[1] To raise money for its development, the US government almost immediately ordered land sales in the northern part of Alabama Territory. In 1811, the land office was moved from Nashville to Huntsville, enticing many people from the eastern states to buy land in the Tennessee Valley. Hunt's Spring and the surrounding acreage were bought at a price of twenty-three dollars an acre by the influential Georgian capitalist LeRoy Pope. As a result of his efforts, the settlement was selected as county seat and its name changed to Twickenham—after the English town his forefathers came from. This name, however, never became popular. And in 1811, the territorial legislature decided to revert to the old name, Huntsville. In 1814, Pope's house was completed on the city's highest hill, a site that provided him with a view over the growing community.

Soon, Huntsville became a frontier metropolis—a flourishing cultural, commercial, and social center of "King Cotton's" realm. One thousand pounds of cotton per acre could be consistently harvested by the farmers of Madison County. The high cotton price was the financial backbone of a prospering city. The streets of Huntsville were dotted with the small

---

[1] Ibid., 12.

offices of cotton merchants, lawyers, and bankers, most of which were located on the west side of the square facing the courthouse. This area became known as "Cotton Row".[2] Farmers brought cotton by wagon and cart to these merchants to be classified for staple and grade and would then sell to the highest

bidder. The town's economy was so dependent on cotton that the entire west side of the square was reserved for cotton wagons and carts.

The frontier character of the town during the antebellum period can be seen by the ratio of male to female population, then almost two to one. In 1825, 308 males were counted to 170 females. A two-story brick courthouse was completed in 1818.[3] Today, you will find its attractive modern counterpart on the same site, which is still the center of the county and city governmental affairs. Around the marketplace "a city of stone and brick" replaced the old wooden construction; it soon covered sixty acres.[4]

The wealthy cotton planters started building distinctive plantation style houses with slave quarters out back; French Empire furniture and fifteenth-century silver-threaded embroidery can still be seen in some of these residences. A weekly paper provided information, a bank the necessary credits for the flourishing plantations and farms. The intellectuals of the city formed a masonic lodge, the theater enthusiasts a thespian, and the music lovers a Hayden Society.

The elegance and fine proportions of Greek revival architecture were introduced to Huntsville by Virginia-born architect George Steele, who had lived in this city since 1818. His conceptions materialized in numerous public and private commissions; among them we have to mention the second courthouse (demolished before 1914) and the First Alabama Bank building (still in use), which he completed in 1840. Fortunately, several Steele-designed private homes can still be seen in the Twickenham District. In 1819, when Alabama progressed from territorial status to statehood as the twenty-second state of the Union, Huntsville was chosen as the temporary capital. Here, Alabama's first constitution was drafted, its first governor inaugurated, and its first legislature convened.

It was vital for the town's economic survival to ship its cotton down

---

[2] Ibid., 14.
[3] Ibid., 23.
[4] Ibid., 26.

the Tennessee River to New Orleans. Therefore, in 1831, the Indian Creek canal was opened from Hunt's Spring to Triana on the Tennessee River. Transportation over land was possible along the Meridian Road, which connects the city to Ditto Landing, a point on the river where John Ditto had established a trading post and ferry service in 1802. Around 1823, James White and other Huntsville businessmen established here a Southern salt monopoly, and the area also became known as Whitesburg. Today, the landing is a convenient yacht harbor. A nine-foot navigable channel makes the Tennessee River an important part of the Southern transport system. The port of Mobile can now be reached by the Tennessee-Tombigbee Waterway.

In 1855, the Memphis and Charleston Railroad was completed. Several years later during the Civil War, the Union generals recognized its strategic importance for the Confederate War effort. And on April 11, 1862, Federal troops under General Mitchell took the city by surprise. As the battle zone was near, Huntsville became a bedroom city and a communications center for the Union forces.[5] However, guerilla attacks constantly harassed the Union troops. One of the leaders was "Morgan the Raider," who had spent his childhood in Huntsville. The hostilities ceased for Huntsville on Monte Sano, its beloved mountain, which provides a fantastic view of the city.

There, on May 11, 1865, the 25th Alabama Battalion was finally forced to surrender. However, twenty-two years later, Monte Sano saw the triumph of the New South—on its summit the greatest hotel of the Tennessee Valley, a majestic 233-room Queen Anne style hotel. The Monte Sano Hotel was opened in June 1887. It was built by the Northern Alabama Improvement Company, which hoped to attract wealthy men for the benefit of local business. Many prominent personalities signed their names in the register, including William H. Vanderbilt, William Waldorf Astor, Walter Damrosch, Jay Gould, and Helen Keller. The hotel succeeded in gaining the city a wide reputation as a health resort before it was sold and dismantled in 1944.[6]

The Monte Sano Hotel, a 233-room resort, opened on the summit of

---

[5] Ibid., 32.
[6] Elfriede Richter-Haaser, "History of Madison County," Madison County Alabama Government, January 2000, 4.

Monte Sano, Madison County, in June 1887. The hotel and its mineral springs drew many wealthy residents from Huntsville and other cities. It closed in 1900 and was demolished in 1944 after many years of decline.[7]

The Monte Sano Hotel

(Picture courtesy of The Huntsville Journal, Friday, April 10, 1905. Consent from Huntsville Public Library Special Collections.)

EARLY HISTORY OF HUNTSVILLE

Who was the first white man to settle in Madison County is yet a question to be considered. But g"Ditto's Landing" (Cherokee-Old-Fields or Whitesburg) some years before Huntsville was located in its present home. That John Hunt was the first white man to build his cabin on the banks of the "Big Spring" is historically settled.

Hunt's cabin was situated on the slope of the bluff overlooking the spring, at the point now the southwest corner of the intersection of Bank Street and Oak Avenue, on the property occupied by the residence of Mr. Frank Murphy. Incidents and circumstances attending Hunt's journey to

---

[7] Ibid., 7.

8 Ibid

the Big Spring confirm the belief that there were white settlers in Madison County, north of Huntsville, before the arrival of John Hunt.

Judge Taylor, in his letters dealing with early life in Madison County, tells us that Joseph and Isaac Criner, accompanied by Stephen McBroom, explored the northern part of the county in 1804 and built a hut on the banks of a stream, now known as Mountain Fork of Flint River. Isaac Criner was personally known to Judge Taylor, and in his letters, he gave us Mr. Criner's narrative of the events of those early days in his own words. In substance, Mr. Criner said, "In the early part of 1805 he and Joseph, his brother, came to Mountain Fork and built a cabin for Joseph's family, then one for himself." Shortly after the erection of these cabins, John Hunt and a man named Bean came to their cabins and spent the night, continuing their journey the next morning. Hunt and Bean came from the north of what is now New Market, along a trail that is now the Winchester, Tennessee, road. They had heard of the Big Spring and of the abundance of big game in its vicinity. In a few weeks, Bean returned and stated he was going back to what is now Bean Creek, near Salem, Tennessee, but that Hunt was going to locate at the Big Spring and would return and bring his family.

Mr. Criner also tells us that, in 1805, several families came into the county from north of New Market, along the same course traversed by Hunt; among them were the Walkers, the Davises, the McBrooms, and the Reeses. These new wealthy and cultured slave owners sent word back to their former friends and neighbors of the unusual fertility of the soil, the beauty of the country, and the wonderful Big Spring. And in 1806, large numbers of home seekers began to come into the county from Middle and East Tennessee and Georgia[8]

These pioneers were of the types usually found on unsettled frontiers "the advance guard of civilization" known as "squatters." They were a very thrifty lot, and at the government land sales in 1809, many were able to buy the tracts upon which they had "squatted" and made their homes. As a whole, they were an honest, law-abiding people, modest in their desires and customs, living peaceably without law or government for some years.

Between 1805 and 1809, wealthy and cultured slave owners came into the county in large numbers from North Carolina, Georgia, and Virginia.

[8] Ibid

Soon, this class outnumbered the pioneers. These later settlers bought large tracts of land at the sales in 1809. In coming into the county, the settlers from North Carolina and Virginia moved along the then western border of civilized customs and cultivated lands into West Georgia and Middle Tennessee, till they reached the Tennessee River, which they crossed near the Georgia line.[9]

December 23, 1809, the territorial legislature passed an act, that "William Dickson, Edward Ward, Louis Winston, Alex Gilbreath, and Peter Perkins of Madison County, be elected commissioners, for the purpose of fixing on the most convenient place for establishing the public

buildings in the said county, and they, or a majority of them, shall have power to procure, by purchase or otherwise, not less than thirty, nor more than one hundred acres of land, at the most which shall be laid out in half-acre lots, reserving three acres for public buildings, and sold at public auction, on twelve months' credit."[10]

The money was to be applied by said commissioners toward defraying the expenses of erecting the public buildings of the county. For the quarter section of land containing the big spring, there was no competition at the land sales of 1809, and LeRoy Pope paid over $823 per acre. At that time, there were two or three hundred inhabitants, scattered over the ground now occupied by Huntsville. The town was first laid out in 1810, and its plan was probably agreed upon between Pope and the commissioners. There were four half-acre lots in each square, and about sixty acres of ground were embraced in the plan.

Pope was a wise and liberal man. The Spring Bluff determined the angle of the streets, which are thirty-four degrees from the true meridian. The first survey of the town was probably the work of John W. Leake.

Hunter Peel came into Huntsville in 1816. The original plan of the town was not recorded and is not extant. The plat thought to be the original plan was drawn by Hunter Peel, by order of the trustees of the Pope donation, in 1821, and still exists.

After the town was first laid out, the commissioners, who all lived in the neighborhood of the Big Spring, purchased thirty acres from Mr. Pope, paying the nominal price of seventy-five dollars. This deed was not

---

[9] Richter-Haaser, "History of Madison County," 15.
[10] Ibid., 18.

recorded until 1815. They selected the south half of the town, the line running through the court house square. This portion of the town was sold rapidly in half-acre lots, bringing from two to five hundred dollars each. Ten thousand dollars was realized and applied to Huntsville, Alabama, now stands and, for his role in the establishment and early growth of that city, has been called the "Father of Huntsville."[11]

Pope was born on January 30, 1765, in Northumberland County, Virginia, the son of LeRoy Pope Sr., and Elizabeth Mitchell. He was educated in his home state and moved with his parents to Amherst County, Virginia. He is said to have served in the American Revolution and was present at the siege and battle of Yorktown, but no official documentation of this service exists.

In 1790, Pope and a host of friends and relatives removed to the town of Petersburg, in Elbert County, Georgia, where he was a tobacco planter. In 1809, he was among the first wave of wealthy settlers to Madison County, Mississippi Territory (now Alabama). He acquired a large tract of land which included the highly sought-after Big Spring, where pioneer John Hunt had settled in 1805. Hunt, like many other squatters, could not afford to purchase his land.

Pope was successful in petitioning the territorial legislature to select his land as the site of Madison County's seat of government. He named the new town Twickenham after the home in England of his distant relative Alexander Pope. In 1811, the town was renamed Huntsville in honor of the pioneer Hunt.[12]

LeRoy Pope's mansion, called Poplar Grove, was erected in 1814, in time to entertain General Andrew Jackson on his return home from the Battle of Horseshoe Bend. It was one of the earliest brick structures in Alabama and remains a prominent Huntsville landmark atop Echols Hill in the Twickenham Historic District.[13] It was restored in the early twenty-first century.

---

[11] Ibid., 34.

[12] Ibid., 36.

[13] Ibid., 43.

Leroy Pope Mansion.

(Photo by Rev. Isaiah Robinson)

Pope was a wealthy and successful planter and was active in the early government and civic leadership of Huntsville and Madison County. He presided as chief justice of the first county court and was among the founders of the First <u>Episcopal</u> Church in Huntsville, organized in 1830.

He was named by the legislature as a commissioner for the Planters' and Merchants' Bank of Huntsville, Alabama's first banking corporation, and for the Indian Creek Navigation Company.

He was married to Judith Sale, daughter of Cornelius Sale and Jane Dawson of <u>Amherst County, Virginia</u>. His daughter Matilda Pope married <u>John Williams Walker</u>, who became Alabama's first <u>senator</u> and was the mother of <u>Confederate</u> Secretary of War and <u>Brigadier General LeRoy Pope Walker</u>, <u>Confederate States Senator Richard Wilde Walker</u>; <u>United States Representative Percy Walker</u>, and several other children. Another daughter, Maria Pope, married Thomas George Percy Sr., and was the ancestor of such notables as Senator <u>LeRoy Percy</u> of <u>Mississippi</u>, the poet <u>William Alexander Percy</u>, Senator <u>Charles H. Percy</u> of <u>Illinois</u>, and the author <u>Walker Percy</u>.

During the original Madison County Land Sales of 1809, LeRoy Pope of Petersburg, Georgia, secured, among other purchases, a majority of Section 36, Township 3, Range 1 West, the site of the future town of Twickenham. Pope created Poplar Grove Plantation on this site and erected his home in 1814 in time to entertain General Andrew Jackson on his return home from the Battle of Horseshoe Bend. The residence was among the earliest brick structures in Alabama. The Pope Mansion was built on top of Echols Hill and, from it, one could see all over the city.

Inherited by his son, William H. Pope, the mansion was sold in 1848 to Dr. Charles Hays Patton, who commissioned George Steele to add the handsome classical revival portico. Nearby during the Civil War, Federal forces built an earthen breastwork to defend the eastern approaches to the city. Pope died in Huntsville on June 17, 1844, and is buried in <u>Maple Hill Cemetery</u>.

3

HOW IT ALL BEGAN FOR THE AFRICAN BAPTIST CHURCH IN HUNTSVILLE, ALABAMA

Slaves in American were brought from many of the areas in Africa. Slaves in Virginia date back to 1619, when many of the slaves were brought from Angola and the Western Coast of Africa. Between 1525 and 1866, <u>12.5 million people</u> were kidnapped from Africa and sent to the Americas through the transatlantic slave trade. Upon reaching the New World, some 3.9 million of the 10.7 million who survived the harrowing two-month journey were enslaved in the United States.

William Harris's father was among the slaves brought into Virginia and was purchased by John Harris. Many of the slaves took the last name of their slave owners. William was born in Virginia; he, along with other family members, belonged to slave master Harris and his wife, Milly. According to deeds, census records, and yearly returns, the Harrises, along with their slaves, moved to the Big Creek area of Oglethorpe County, Georgia, the county of the area of Walton, Georgia. Young William Harris grew to be an outstanding man and was very interested in knowing about Christianity.

The traditional African religions (or traditional beliefs and practices of African people) are a set of highly diverse beliefs that include various ethnic religions. Generally, these traditions are oral rather than scriptural and include belief in a number of higher and lower gods, sometimes including a supreme creator, belief in spirits, veneration of the dead, and use of magic and traditional African medicine.[14] Most of the religions can be described as animism with various polytheistic and pantheistic aspects. The role of humanity is generally seen as one of harmonizing nature with the supernatural.

According to Luzira, A religion researcher. According to Luzira, animism is the only religion that can claim to have originated in Africa. Other religions found in Africa have their origins in other parts of the world." Because the Islamic religion had begun to spread into West Africa, perhaps as many as 20 percent of the slaves brought to America were Muslims.

The original religion of the African people, however, was animism (the worship of spirits), and there is no doubt that most of the slaves were animists. The origin of African religion holds the view that African traditional religion (ATR) originated from fetish (the worship of inanimate things and animals). People believed that every external object in nature possessed life and magical powers. The Portuguese word *feitico* means "charm" and was applied to "relics" (part of the body, dress, and so on).[15]

African religions' customs before Christianity involved ancestor worship. Central to traditional African religion was respect for ancestors. Was God the Supreme Being? Christian missionaries in Africa often thought the people served multiple gods. As for the African spirit world, spirits inhabited the world, along with the living.

Religion, particularly Christianity, has played an outsize role in African American history. While most Africans brought to the New World to be slaves were not Christians when they arrived, many of them and their descendants embraced Christianity, finding comfort in the biblical message of spiritual equality and deliverance. In post-Civil War America, a burgeoning black church played a key role in strengthening African American communities and in providing key support to the civil rights movement. At the time John Harris arrived in Oglethorpe County, the

---

[14] James Benson Sellers, *Slavery in Alabama* (Tuscaloosa: University of Alabama Press, 1994), 21.

[15] Peter Kolchin, *American Slavery: 1619–1877* (New York: Hill and Wang, 2003), 19.

main cash crop was cotton. The years during the Civil War were very prosperous for the residents of Oglethorpe County.

It was during this time that the plantation system was well established in Georgia. Just prior to their arrival, several early churches were formed. Indians were still a big concern for John and his neighbors. Many congregations met in the homes of its members. It is thought that they attended Big Creek Primitive Baptist Church. We know the Bolling family records show that members of Milly's family were some of the first members.

The church was close to their home. Milly was a charter member of Sorrells Springs Primitive Baptist church in Walton County. These churches taught the Primitive Baptist doctrine and faith.

John would allow his slaves to attend church services with him and his family, where the slaves would sit in the back of the church or in the balcony. Many of his slaves accepted Christ and were given permission by the slave owners to be baptized by the white ministers in the Primitive Baptist faith.

William Harris studied the word of God through the Harrises. He grew in the Word of God, and the slave owner gave permission for him to become a minister after the calling of God was on him. He was ordained by the white elders and given the title of Elder William Harris. There were other slaves on that plantation and other plantations, and Elder William Harris was given permission to preach the Word of God in a non-rebellious manner to other slaves. This occurred mostly at night in areas designated by the slave owners.

Elder William Harris parents had died, and he had his own family, who also accepted Christ and adopted this religion that was new to them. Among the most active was his grandson Bartley Harris. Bartley Harris was baptized by his grandfather and the white minister and was also ordained an elder of the Primitive Baptist faith.

In the early 1800s in Georgia, certain areas were becoming more populated. The land was showing the potential of its yield, and plantations were numerous. The growing problem resulting from the planter's life was slavery. A few doctors, traveling over many miles, provided what health care there was at that time. Times, though good, were very hard.

With the death of William Harris's father and the utilization of slaves in Virginia and North Carolina. John Harris, prior to his death, gave young William Harris and his family members, including his grandson, their freedom papers and freed them from slavery. However, they remained on the plantation assisting Mrs. Milly Harris with chores that had to be done to keep the plantation functioning.

Elder William Harris, having become so acquainted with the Primitive Baptist faith, left the plantation and traveled to various plantations, preaching the Gospel as a free man. Eventually he traveled from Georgia to Huntsville, Alabama, because of the growth of the area and the great supply of work. He obtained work with the various slave owners there and persuaded the slave owners to allow their slaves to worship with him in the worshipping of the Gospel of Jesus Christ. They were assured that the worship was not of a rebellious nature but simply to teach and preach the Word of God.

Elder William Harris was granted permission to meet with slaves at night in what was known as the "Old Georgia Graveyard."[16] There, slaves would worship and praise God. Many times, they would cover their heads with pots and other materials to keep from causing a lot of noise with their worship.

In 1808, Harris informally organized the African Baptist Church, and congregants met in the graveyard for service.

While Harris was working in the community doing various odd jobs, he met Leroy Pope, and Pope took favor to him. On September 3, 1818, the Huntsville City Commissioners purchased two acres of land from LeRoy Pope for a "burying ground" for slaves. This cemetery was located within the northeast quarter of Section 1, Township 4, Range 1 West of the Base Meridian. It was affectionately known as "Georgia" within the black community. The cemetery continued to be used from 1818 until 1870, when Glenwood Cemetery was designated as the city's burial ground for African Americans. No known records have survived.

The Huntsville City Commissioners, along with Leroy Pope, gave full permission to Elder William Harris to hold worship services there in

---

[16] Kenneth Oster, *The Examiner: Church in Society* (Washington, DC: Association for Study of African Baptist Church, 1987), 43.

that graveyard and to build a structure that would allow them a place to formally worship in.

In 1820 Elder William Harris formally organized the African Baptist Church which was approved by the city. The cemetery continued to be used from 1818 until 1870, when Glenwood Cemetery was designated as the city's burial ground for African Americans. No known records have survived. Instituted in 1808 by enslaved blacks and formally organized in 1820, the African Baptist Church (St. Bartley Primitive Baptist Church of Huntsville, Alabama,) exemplifies 206 years of black religious independence. It was originally located outside the city limits of Huntsville near present-day Governors Drive and Madison Street, among the tombstones, dogwoods, and flowering trees of the Old Georgia Graveyard—a slave graveyard and the only land that enslaved blacks could claim.

The original congregation appears to have been composed of slaves transported by their owners from Georgia to northern Alabama. St. Bartley, initially called the African Huntsville Baptist Church, is recognized widely as being Alabama's oldest black church.

Early worship services at African Huntsville Baptist Church occurred at night so that members could express freely their religious feelings and their desires for freedom and self-expression, which were outlawed in Alabama at that time.

Although the specific date is unknown, the African Huntsville Baptist Church erected a small church edifice in the graveyard. Shepherded by Elder William Harris, a free black man, the church flourished, subsequently joining, in 1821, the Flint River Association in communion with other churches located along the Tennessee River. Although ran by whites, the association never attempted to impose its supervision on African Huntsville.

As a consequence, the church congregation grew. The African Huntsville Baptist Church numbered 265 by 1840 and 432 in 1849. With the growth of the church and its increasing influence, Elder Harris sent for his grandson Elder Bartley Harris and his family to come to Huntsville to assist him in this great work. Elder Bartley Harris joined Elder William Harris, and he and his family settled in the area today known as Harvest.

Since blacks could not own land, the Harris family served as sharecroppers on the property until, later, they became owners of the property. Elder Bartley Harris proved to be a great asset to the church in assisting Elder William Harris, and the two of them were widely recognized for their outstanding character and integrity among the whites.

Slaves and free blacks, however, lived in an increasingly dangerous world in northern Alabama toward the end of the antebellum period. As the South moved closer to disunion and war, the Huntsville City Council restricted access to the city for any black citizen who arrived in Huntsville after 1832. Nevertheless, black men represented African Huntsville at annual association meetings as designated in the 1814 Flint River Association Constitution and continued to do so from 1821 to 1866.

Historians attribute this evenhanded dealing by the association to its doctrinal stance. The Flint River Association held that "the merits of Christ [grace] alone are sufficient for the salvation of sinners, unaided by human effort."[17]

Elder William Harris preached that "man is saved by grace alone and faith in Jesus Christ" as he led the church into the Primitive Baptist fold. Primitive Baptists believe in salvation by the grace of God and that scripture alone should guide one's faith and life. In keeping with this firm belief in scripture, they believed that all men are equal in the eyes of God: "There is neither Jew nor Greek, there is neither slave nor free, there is neither male nor female; for you are all one in Christ Jesus" (Galatians 3:28 NKJ).

Eventually, the slaves were able to erect a building within the graveyard, and that building was known as the Huntsville African Baptist Church.

(Picture courtesy of the Southern Advocate, August 19, 1820.
From the Huntsville Public Library Special Collections.)

Despite the restrictions placed upon the slaves, the church grew and spread its roots throughout Madison County during slavery. It is commonly supposed that trustworthy slave preachers were allowed to travel from

---

[17] Minutes of a meeting of Flint River Primitive Baptist Association, Constitution, 1821.

plantation to plantation within a given area for purposes of preaching the Gospel of Jesus Christ and that such preaching was permitted among the slaves. Elder William Harris had the opportunity to establish a fellowship with men such as Elder Henry Burwell, who established the Beaver Dam Primitive Baptist Church in the mid-1800s. It is not known what this church was called when it was first established. But given the past practices of both slaves and free blacks, that name was somehow associated with their African heritage. These two pastors, plus the pastors of the Indian Creek Primitive Baptist Church and the Meridianville Bottom Primitive Church, organized the Indian Creek Primitive Baptist Association five years after the effective date of the Emancipation Proclamation in January 1865.

The Indian Creek Primitive Baptist Association was organized on Saturday before the third Sunday in September—September 17, 1870. The organizational effort was accomplished in an open field, under a tree, and near a stream located nine miles north of Huntsville, Alabama.[18]

Elder William Harris, founding pastor of the Huntsville African Baptist Church in 1820, which is now called Saint Bartley Primitive Baptist Church, encouraged three other churches to unite under the bounds of a common faith and doctrine for the purpose of organizing an Association of Black Primitive Baptists. The four churches who participated in the organizational meeting were Saint Bartley, Meridianville Bottom, Beaver Dam, and Indian Creek Primitive Baptist Churches.

Prior to the Civil War that led to the emancipation of African slaves in America, Elder William Harris was a member of the White Flint River Primitive Baptist Association.

However, after President Abraham Lincoln signed the Emancipation Proclamation on January 1, 1863, circumstances encountered in the White Flint River Primitive Baptist Association, the freedom realized by slaves as a result of the Emancipation Proclamation, and the divine providence of God moved Elder William Harris to seek a fresh direction for the former slaves in North Alabama. Consequently, contact was established, in 1869, with the Big Harpeth United Primitive Baptist Association of Nashville, Tennessee, for the purpose of forming a Black Primitive Baptist Association.

---

[18] Minutes of the Indian Creek Primitive Baptist Association, September 17, 1870.

The Indian Creek Primitive Baptist Association was formally organized by Elder Thomas Williamson, Moderator of the Big Harpeth United Primitive Baptist Association, Nashville, Tennessee. He was aided by Elder Eli Grant, a member of the same association. The name "Indian Creek" was adopted because, in the place where the organizational meeting was held, there was a flowing stream of water nearby that was frequently utilized by Indians as their campground as they traveled through this region of the country. Presently, the stream is known as the Indian Creek.

The names of men who have willingly and gracefully accepted the leadership of this association from inception to the present include Elder William Harris, first moderator; Elders B. L. Chapman, John Malone, J. S. Bailey, Jerome Sales, Elias Patton, J. M. Smith, Wesley Batts, Eli Moore, W. M. Mastin, Amos Robinson, Ezell Tibbs, Eugene Lewis, and Robert Rogers Sr.; and the current moderator, Mylon L. Burwell.

The 1860 United States Census indicated that Elder William Harris was seventy-eight years of age and Elder Bartley Harris was fifty years of age.[19] As Elder William Harris became ill and died in 1872, no trace of his burial has ever been found due to a lack of a headstone marking. More likely, his grave still exists under the present site of the Huntsville Hospital. In 1872 after the death of Elder William Harris, Elder Bartley Harris took the responsibility as pastor of the church.

The Alabama enacted law of 1833 prohibited slaves from assembling in large numbers, even for spiritual worship, unless a white man was present to regulate their discussions. Freedom talks and issues of God-given equality and rights were outlawed. Yet the message of hope went out. They found ways to conduct night worship services, and they developed spiritual songs and hymns to communicate deep, meaningful messages to slaves from the Old Georgia Graveyard.

Around this time, under the leadership of Elder Bartley Harris, a small building was erected in the cemetery for use as a black church, though the presence of a white person was still required before services could be held.

The pastor, Elder Bartley Harris, who shared his surname with his grandfather, Elder William Harris, preached sermons of salvation. Ironically, while the white community did not trust Elder Bartley Harris

---

[19] 1860 Census Madison County, Alabama, transcribed by Linda Hardiman Smith, June 7, 1860, 16.

to preach sermons on his own accord, many white people trusted him to hide their valuables—silver, money, pictures, artifacts, gold, weapons, and other things of value—when the Union forces occupied Huntsville during the Civil War.

As the Civil War increased in its ardor and victories, the Union Army moved into Huntsville and took over many of the homes and buildings and their belongings. The Union Army found the blacks worshipping in a building in the Georgia Graveyard and took control of the building. They tore down the structure and used the wood to build headquarters there in Huntsville. What remained of the original church building was destroyed by fire during the Union occupation after they failed to obtain information from Elder Bartley Harris concerning the valuables he had hidden.

On the morning of April 11, 1862, Union troops led by General Ormsby M. Mitchel seized Huntsville in order to sever the Confederacy's rail communications and gain access to the Memphis & Charleston Railroad. Huntsville was the control point for the western division of the Memphis & Charleston, and by controlling this railroad, the Union had struck a major blow to the Confederacy.

During the first occupation, Union officers occupied many of the larger homes in the city, while the enlisted soldiers camped mainly on the outskirts. In the initial occupation, the Union troops searched for both Confederate troops hiding in the town and weapons. Since they occupied the city, treatment of Huntsville was relatively civil. However, residents of the nearby towns did not fare as well.

Union troops were forced to retreat only a few months later, but they returned to Huntsville in the fall of 1863 and, thereafter, used the city as a base of operations for the war, except during the last month of 1864. While many homes and villages in the surrounding countryside were burned in retaliation for the active guerrilla warfare in the area, Huntsville itself survived because it housed Union Army troops. When the soldiers questioned Elder Bartley Harris, he refused to tell them if and where he had hidden the valuables of the whites, so in retribution, the soldiers burned the little church to the ground.

After the war, the valuables were returned to the citizens by Elder Harris. He could easily have sold those valuables during the war to finance his escape to the North, but Elder Harris chose to remain with his small congregation. The war dealt a heavy blow to the black congregation when the church was burned by Union soldiers during Huntsville's occupation.

After the Civil War, the structure was rebuilt in 1872 with money appropriated by the United States Congress. People or organizations who suffered financial losses during the conflict and who could prove they were not sympathetic to the Confederacy were entitled to compensation from the Federal government. President Ulysses S. Grant signed the appropriation papers authorizing the transfer of those funds, and especially for the rebuilding of the church. At this time, money was saved, and they continue to meet in the graveyard. The rebuilding of the church was done and was rededicated in 1872 in a nearby location known as Oak Avenue.

At this time, the name was changed from the Huntsville African Baptist Church to the St. Bartley Primitive Baptist Church, out of respect for their pastor who was said to be a saintly person and to have baptized some three thousand people in his lifetime. Elder Harris and the African Baptist Church, based on the reassessment of the building, was awarded approximately $5,000 by President Grant for the rebuilding of the church according the US Claims Court.[20]

With the beginnings of religion in Alabama, log and clapboard churches were among the most important buildings in the Alabama Territory in the early to mid-1800s. In addition to providing space for worshipping, they were often multipurpose buildings used as schools and for community events.

In the nearly two hundred years since Alabama became a state in 1819, many of those buildings were lost to age, progress, and the Civil War. But incredibly, Alabamians have preserved dozens of those early churches.

Although there were plenty of outlaws among the pioneers settling the Alabama Territory, they were far outnumbered by law-abiding, churchgoing citizens. Early parishioners were mostly Presbyterians, Methodists, and Baptists, with fewer numbers of Episcopalians, Jews, and Catholics. Methodists and Baptists established their first congregations in 1808, according to historian Wayne Flynt in an article in the *Encyclopedia of Alabama.*

Before long, some Baptists would split from the church to form the

---

[20] Library of Congress, "US Court of Claims," Washington, DC., October–November 1903.

Primitive Baptist Church. Before the Civil War, women and black people were not welcome in the pulpit. As slaves they always sat separately from white congregants, and women sometimes had separate seating from men.

The Civil War changed the course of religion in Alabama. Many Methodist, Baptist, Presbyterian, and Christian churches split from their national denominations over the issue of slavery, forming Southern divisions. Afterward, the human and financial costs of the conflict halted progress on most church projects such as new colleges. With the burning of the church building in the Georgia Graveyard by the Union Army, the slaves continued to worship on the grounds of the graveyard and buried their dead. Graves were marked with field stones. The graves are located on the grounds of a former log church built for worship. For slaves, even the practice of having funerals and burying their dead was an act of resistance. They could only have a limited number of people at funerals and no markers. They attempted to ease the psychological pain by not remembering. At the end of slavery, they stopped talking about their past.

An enslaved burial spot can include nondescript rocks clustered together or land marked by depressions over time. When you destroy these graves, it was a case of erasing the people again.

Under these early codes, slaves had virtually no legal rights. In most areas, they could be executed for crimes that were not capital offenses for whites. Their testimony was restricted in legal cases and could not be used either for or against whites. Trials of slaves were usually by special courts. Slaves could not own property, move about without consent of their owners, or legally marry.

Elder William Harris was the First Moderator of the Indian Creek Primitive Baptist Association. Elder William Harris served the Huntsville African Baptist Church as pastor and slaves they always sat separately from white congregants, and women sometimes had separate seating from men.

The Civil War changed the course of religion in Alabama. Many Methodist, Baptist, Presbyterian, and Christian churches split from their national denominations over the issue of slavery, forming Southern divisions. Afterward, the human and financial costs of the conflict halted progress on most church projects such as new colleges. With the burning of the church building in the Georgia Graveyard by the Union Army, the slaves continued to worship on the grounds of the graveyard and buried their dead. Graves were marked with field stones. The graves are located on the grounds of a former log church built for worship. For slaves, even the practice of having funerals and burying their dead was an act of resistance. "They could only have a limited number of people at funerals and no markers." They attempted to ease the psychological pain by not remembering. At the end of slavery, they stopped talking about their past.

An enslaved burial spot can include nondescript rocks clustered together or land marked by depressions over time. "When you destroy these graves, it was a case of erasing the people again."

Under these early codes, slaves had virtually no legal rights. In most areas, they could be executed for crimes that were not capital offenses for whites. Their testimony was restricted in legal cases and could not be used either for or against whites. Trials of slaves were usually by special courts. Slaves could not own property, move about without consent of their owners, or legally marry.

Elder William Harris was the First Moderator of the Indian Creek Primitive Baptist Association. Elder William Harris served the Huntsville African Baptist Church as pastor.

ST. BARTLEY PRIMITIVE BAPTIST CHURCH: HISTORICAL PERSPECTIVE SUMMATION REFLECTION

On September 3, 1818, the Huntsville City Commissioners purchased two acres of land from Leroy Pope for a "burying ground" for slaves. This land was a cemetery and was located within the northeast quarter of Section 1, Township 4, and Range 1 West of the Base Meridian. It was affectionately known as "Georgia" or the "Old Georgia Graveyard" within the black community. The cemetery continued to be used from 1818 until 1870, when Glenwood Cemetery was designated as the city's burial ground for African Americans. It was here at "Old Georgian Graveyard" that slaves would go to pray and hold religious services of worship to God. The "Old Georgian Graveyard" was located where the present-day Huntsville Hospital and Medical Area of Madison Street and St. Clair Avenue can now be found.

I learned more about the "Georgian Graveyard" from the late Deacon T. E. Jackson' Deacon John W. Laughinghouse Sr.; Deacon Willie B. Moore; the late Elder W. H. Burwell; and the late Elder W. M. Mastin. Every aspect of information from each of them was a learning and challenging experience. It made you love and appreciate the St. Bartley Church even more, for it was from that graveyard that the present-day St. Bartley Primitive Baptist Church was born.

Instituted in 1808 by enslaved blacks, St. Bartley Primitive Baptist Church of Huntsville, Alabama, exemplifies 206 years of black religious independence. It was located originally outside the city limits of Huntsville near present-day Governors Drive and Madison Street, among the tombstones, dogwoods, and flowering trees of the Old Georgia Graveyard—a slave graveyard and the only land that enslaved blacks could claim. The original congregation appears to have been composed of slaves transported by their owners from Georgia to northern Alabama. St. Bartley, initially called the African Huntsville Church, is recognized widely as being Alabama's oldest black church.

Early worship services at African Huntsville Church occurred at night so that members could express freely their religious feelings and their desires for freedom and self-expression, which were outlawed in Alabama at that time. Although the specific date is unknown, the African Huntsville Church erected a small church edifice in the graveyard. Shepherded by William Harris, a free black man, the church flourished, subsequently joining, in 1821, the Flint River Association in communion with other churches located along the Tennessee River. Although run by whites, the association never attempted to impose its supervision on African Huntsville Church. As a consequence, the church congregation grew. It numbered 265 by 1840 and 432 in 1849.

Slaves and free blacks, however, lived in an increasingly dangerous world in northern Alabama toward the end of the antebellum period. As the South moved closer to disunion and war, the Huntsville City Council restricted access to the city for any black citizen who arrived in Huntsville after 1832. Many of the slaves in the congregation were workers for the whites who lived in Huntsville in the downtown district in quarters behind their owners' huge lavish homes. They were permitted to attend worship at the Georgia Graveyard. Nevertheless, black men represented African

Huntsville at annual association meetings as designated in the 1814 Flint River Association Constitution and continued to do so from 1821 to 1866.

Elder William Harris, the founder, did outstanding work and leadership for the church and made friends with the many whites in Huntsville. Other free slaves came from Georgia and South Carolina to Huntsville and also worshipped at the Georgia Graveyard. The material for the small building was mostly donated by whites in sympathy with Elder Harris and the slaves.

Elder William Harris died in 1872 and was buried in the Georgia Graveyard. However, there was no grave marker for his grave. When the Georgia Graveyard was abolished, many of the graves were transposed to the new Glenwood Cemetery in Huntsville. However, those graves without a marker were left in the old Georgia Graveyard site. Elder William Harris's grave was not moved, as no marker was there to identify his grave.

Elder Bartley Harris, the grandson to Elder William Harris, was from South Carolina. He and his family relocated to Huntsville and worshipped in the Georgia Graveyard. With the death of Elder William Harris, Elder Bartley Harris was elected as pastor in 1872. He led the church very successfully.

Historians attribute this evenhanded dealing by the Flint River Association to its doctrinal stance. The Flint River Association held that "the merits of Christ (grace) alone are sufficient for the salvation of sinners, unaided by human effort." Elder Bartley Harris preached that man is saved by grace alone as he led the church into the Primitive Baptist fold.

Primitive Baptists believe in salvation by the grace of God and that scriptures alone should guide one's faith and life. In keeping with this firm belief in scriptures, they believed that all men are equal in the eyes of God.

The original church building was destroyed by fire during the Union occupation after the Civil War and was rebuilt in 1872 with money appropriated by the United States Congress. People or organizations who suffered financial losses during the conflict and who could prove they were not sympathetic to the Confederacy were entitled to compensation from the Federal government. President Ulysses S. Grant signed the appropriation papers authorizing the transfer of those funds.

According to the records of *Encyclopedia of Alabama*, slavery existed in Alabama even before it became a state. Beginning in the territorial period in the early nineteenth century, the institution expanded, coinciding with the development and growth of plantation agriculture. Slavery in Alabama and the United States was a labor system that depended upon captive Africans who were held by their owners as legal property in a state of permanent bondage. Most enslaved individuals in Alabama were born into enslavement in other states and brought into the area as part of the South's internal slave trade. Although the living conditions and work required of slaves varied widely across the state, the patterns and variations in Alabama broadly reflected the slave experience elsewhere in the Deep South.

By the antebellum period, Alabama had evolved into a slave society, which is characterized by the proliferation and defense of the institution that shaped much of the state's economy, politics, and culture. The defense of slavery played a significant role in Alabama's secession from the Union in 1861. The collapse of the Confederate States of America and the end of the American Civil War (1861–1865) resulted in the emancipation of the state's enslaved population.

Evangelical Christianity dominated the religious life of Alabama's slave population. During Alabama's territorial period, slaveholders were only marginally interested in efforts to Christianize slaves. Attitudes began to change during the mid-eighteenth century, however, when large percentages of slaves converted to Christianity as a result of the Great Awakening (a period of religious fervor that swept the American colonies in the 1730s and 1740s).

Decades later, during the Second Great Awakening (circa 1790–1840), a brand of evangelical Christianity spread among Southern slaveholders who were inspired by revivals targeting both masters and slaves. Like their white owners, the majority of slaves in Alabama were Baptists and Methodists. In 1808, the African Huntsville Church (St. Bartley) was founded, and by 1849, its membership rolls had swelled to more than four hundred slaves. Similar independent black churches existed elsewhere in Alabama. White churches routinely baptized and extended membership to slaves. Antebellum churches often had segregated seating areas for black worshipers. The spread of evangelical Christianity among slaves was influenced by sermons delivered by preachers who warned slaveholders to promote the faith among their slaves or risk damnation. Slaveholders were equally motivated to spread Christianity among their slaves in response to

Northern abolitionists, who criticized the morality of Christian believers who owned slaves.

The outcome of the American Civil War ended slavery in Alabama. The Thirteenth Amendment permanently abolished slavery in the United States in 1865. Alabama freed people welcomed emancipation but endured continuing hardships because of the prevailing and pervasive racial prejudices of the state's white inhabitants.

A rift formed between what the masters viewed as acceptable worship and what the slaves practiced in secret. Some of the masters didn't like the way slaves carried on. They would turn pots, and tubs down and place their heads under them to keep the sounds of praying and praising God from going out. They would have a good time, shouting, singing, and praying. On a plantation with intolerant masters, slaves often had to go underground to partake in any sort of worship; the oppression that slaves lived under shaped the way they encountered religion.

Scholars have argued in the past that harsh masters and the institution of slavery itself erased any legacy of traditional African religious culture, leaving them to inherit an entirely European-influenced version of Christianity from their masters. However, others have cited evidence of African culture that lingered in the slave community, emphasizing the influence this culture had on Christian slave practices. If one considers slave narratives and records from early black religious communities, it's evident that whites used Christianity as a method of social control among their slaves. Consequently, slaves developed a distinct version of Christianity that fit their own needs, provided a sense of community, and incorporated their old African religious traditions.

Whites did not begin scattered attempts to convert their slaves to Christianity until the early to mid-eighteenth century; this was because whites had hidden agendas. Before these early conversions, masters had been more concerned with economic profit than missionary zeal; they feared that any effort to Christianize slaves would take away valuable time that the slaves could be working in the fields. Masters also feared that, if slaves were capable of conversion, they must in fact have souls and so would need to be set free, since Anglican belief dictated that fellow Christians were not to be enslaved. This fear caused many planters to refuse to let missionaries convert their slaves—given the loss of an extremely valuable financial asset at risk.

Slaves themselves started to realize that church services and sermons were being used as tools to control them. Blacks sat in the gallery behind the whites, and preachers told the congregation to, "Obey yo' master an' yo' missus an' you will always do right.[21] Slave religion differed from what whites had taught them. Masters and overseers had preachers stress the values of obedience and staying in one's place, forcing slaves to hear this message every Sunday and taking away its validity.

Christianity truly rooted itself in the black community as slaves began to discover the Bible for themselves, regardless of whites' efforts to censor the religious material slaves had access to in sermons. Since slaves had to look past the face value of the lessons that white preachers taught them, they had to find a new resource to teach them about the true nature of Christianity. The Bible became the main source of authority in black religion. This emphasis that was placed on the Bible.

The emphasis placed on the Bible made learning to read all that more important among the black community. Despite attempts to prevent reading among the slaves, literacy still existed and allowed identifiable stories like Exodus to be circulated. This story was extremely popular among slaves, who could identify with the Hebrews in bondage. Slaves did not need to be literate to make the connection that an all-powerful and loving God would not have condoned the treatment of his people in slavery.

Since not all slaves could read for themselves, a common way for the message to be spread was through spirituals such as "When Israel Was in Egypt's' Land": "No more shall they in bondage toil, / Let my people go, / Let them come out with Egypt's spoil, / Let my people go." Spirituals were one of the ways that slaves incorporated Biblical stories into their day-to-day activities; they were often sung while working in the fields.[22] Usually, the slave on the plantation who was most knowledgeable or well versed in Bible passages would take charge at these meetings, performing conversions, leading hymns, and singing spirituals which gave vent to their

---

[21] William Warren Rogers, *Alabama: The History of Deep South State* (Tuscaloosa: The University of Alabama Press, 1994), 110.
[22] Ibid.

true feelings. These black preachers, sometimes referred to as chair backs, did not have to censor their petitions for freedom, as long as they were careful to remain undercover.

Some plantations did not permit slaves any form of religious experience—even sitting in the gallery at a white church service. However, many masters did allow slaves to attend white church services, and the slaves would still meet in secret to worship. At these meetings, slaves did indeed diverge from the version of Christianity that introduced them to and had a distinct component to their worship based not only on spiritual well-being but also on their physical bondage in slavery as well.

Through worship, slaves were able to focus on their own needs as people with a shared history and experience. This recognition of a common identity and purpose gave blacks exactly what whites had been trying to prohibit them from forming since the very beginning—a sense of community. The black church was able to provide an outlet for the slaves, where they could escape from the social structure of their normal lives. Every aspect of a slave's life was controlled by their master or overseer—when they woke up in the morning, the amount of work they did, what church service they could attend, where they could sit in the church, and so on. The black church provided an opportunity to escape the rigidness of slavery and gain a sense of control over their own lives.

During black prayer meetings and worship services, slaves experienced an equality they could never experience in the outside world. In a physical sense, many of the usual restrictions the whites imposed on them were absent. They did not have to sit in the back gallery of the church like they did during the majority of white services. They were not watched over by anyone holding a whip and threatening to use it at the slightest sign of laughter or outward emotion. They were not forced to leave the church building before the service ended.

An even more significant aspect of this equality blacks shared in their worship services was a sort of expressive equality. Outside of whites' earshot, slaves could "shout an' pray" for freedom and salvation to their heart's content. They were free to control what was preached and what they chose to listen to. In other words, having their own religious outlets gave slaves a sense of empowerment in a world where they were typically powerless. In preaching and in church life some blacks found channels for self-expression and self-governance. Equality also extended to a spiritual sense of the word, since the Christian belief was that everyone is equal in the eyes of God. Slaves found support for this idea in Bible verses, such as Galatians 3:28, NKJV that claimed, "Ye are all one in Jesus Christ."[23] This sense of equality created an open and accepting atmosphere for slave to worship in.

This aspect led to the birth of the Primitive Baptist Church, Colored, of Huntsville, Alabama. The stipulation of "colored" was used to distinguish it from the White Primitive Baptist Church of Huntsville, Alabama. Later, the "colored church" became known as the African This sense of equality created an open and accepting atmosphere for slave to worship in.

This aspect led to the birth of the Primitive Baptist Church, Colored, of Huntsville, Alabama. The stipulation of "colored" was used to distinguish it from the White Primitive Baptist Church of Huntsville, Alabama. Later, the "colored church" became known as the African Primitive Baptist Church and is presently the Saint Bartley Primitive Baptist Church in Huntsville, Alabama.[24]

---

[23] Zola, Crowell, *Alabama: Free People of Color* (Tuscaloosa: University of Alabama Press, 2003), 40.

[24] Ibid., 43.

THE BEGINNING OF A NEW ERA

In 1872, Elder Bartley Harris became the pastor of the Huntsville African Baptist Church. In 1872, under the leadership of Elder Bartley Harris, the Huntsville African Baptist Church relocated to Oak Avenue, now Gallatin Street, also known as Fountain Row, on the southwest side of Huntsville. The church building was a gray concrete brick building with Gothic windows of ornamental glass and was not only the first but, for many years, also the largest black church in Alabama.

It became known as the "Big Brick." No records list the purchase of the land, but the property was owned by Leroy Pope in 1810.[25]

It burned to the ground in 1866 because the Union soldiers were angry over the hiding of the whites' valuables. The congregation had to meet at the Rust Normal School, which was founded by the Black Methodist Church and is believed to have been located on Franklin Street. The Huntsville African Baptist Church had been awarded approximately $5,000 by President Ulysses Grant during the Civil War, due to its destruction by the Union Army.[26]

---

[25] *Southern Advocate*, Huntsville, June 21, 1844.

[26] Ibid.

During the Civil War, the occupation of Huntsville by the Union soldiers resulted in the destruction by fire of the small church that had been built in the Old Georgia Graveyard.

Elder Bartley Harris Sr., the second pastor of the church, had been approached by white citizens who asked him to hide their personal valuables from the Union troops. Elder Bartley Harris did so. He loaded a wagon of their valuables, which included silver, gold, weapons, pictures, artworks, jewelry, paintings, valuable documents, and many other valuables; covered them in a wagon driven by some mules; and carried the valuables to a safe place. When the soldiers questioned him, he refused to tell them if and where he had hidden the valuables. In retribution, the soldiers burned the little church to the ground. After the war, Elder Bartley Harris returned the valuables to the white citizens and owners.

President Ulysses Grant heard of the soldiers' action and the burning of the building in the cemetery and appropriated money for rebuilding the church. A bigger and better sanctuary was built and rededicated on what was Oak Street and is now Williams Street on Fountain Row in 1872. The church remained on this site for ninety-two years. At this time, the name of the church was changed from Huntsville African Baptist Church to Saint Bartley Primitive Baptist Church, out of respect for the saintly behavior of the pastor, Elder Bartley Harris.[27]

Looking back into the history of the "Georgia Graveyard," the origins of its name are unknown, though it has been suggested it was so named because many of the area's first settlers came there from Georgia. Although the site

---

[27] *Southern Advocate*, June 22, 1844.

had originally been established as a white city cemetery, black people were also buried there even at an early date. The custom of the time, as evidenced by countless cemeteries throughout the South, dictated that both whites and blacks were often buried in the same grounds. Harsh as slavery was, the white masters often felt a paternal instinct toward their slaves, even in death.

The site of the new cemetery, however, proved to be an unfortunate one. Early accounts showed that the area was prone to flooding and was a virtual swamp for much of the time. After only four years, Georgia Cemetery was deemed unsuitable for burial and Leroy Pope sold the city another tract of land, later to become known as Maple Hill Cemetery.

Maple Hill Cemetery is the oldest and largest cemetery in Huntsville, Alabama. Founded on 2 acres (8,000 m²) in about the year 1822, it now encompasses nearly 100 acres and contains over eighty thousand burials. It was added to the Alabama Historical Commission's Historic Cemetery Register in 2008 and to the National Register of Historic Places in 2012. Its occupants include five governors of Alabama, five United States senators, and numerous other figures of local, state, and national note. It is located east of the Twickenham Historic District. In 1873, the cemetery was further expanded through the purchase, from James J. Donegan, of 12.45 acres (50,380 m²) that had previously been a part of the Pope estate. In this new addition were two sections consecrated for religious congregations, a Hebrew burial ground and a Catholic burial ground.[28]

The Alabama Historical Commission is the historic preservation agency for the US state of Alabama.[29] The agency was created by an act of the state legislature in 1966, with a mission of safeguarding Alabama's historic buildings and sites. It consists of twenty members appointed by the state governor or who serve in an official position. The members represent a broad cross section of Alabamians, including architects, historians, archaeologists, and representatives of state universities. The commission is tasked with acquisition and preservation of historic properties and education of the public about historic sites in Alabama.

---

[28] Diane Robey, Dorothy Scott Johnson, John Rison Jones Jr., and Frances C. Roberts, *Maple Hill Cemetery: Phase One* (Huntsville: Huntsville-Madison County Historical Society, 1995).

[29] "Alabama Register of Landmarks and Heritage," Alabama Historical Commission, archived from the original on January 5, 2008, retrieved February 8, 2013.

The original two acres of the cemetery were sold to the city of Huntsville on September 14, 1822 by planter <u>LeRoy Pope</u>. Though early burials are difficult to document, there is substantial evidence that the land had been in use as a cemetery for some time prior to its official establishment. The cemetery was expanded at some point after 1849 to include the two acres on which LeRoy Pope and his family were buried. There are some indications that this land, which had until then remained a part of the Pope estate, may already have been in use as a burial ground.

Leroy Pope was a wealthy and successful planter and was active in the early government and civic leadership of Huntsville and Madison County. During the original Madison County Land Sales of 1809, Leroy Pope secured, among other purchases, a majority of Section 36, Township 3 Range 1 West, the site of the future town of Twickenham, as Huntsville was originally known. And the Maple Hill land was included. Pope created Poplar Grove Plantation on this site and erected his home in 1814, in time to entertain General Andrew Jackson on his return from the Battle of Horseshoe Bend. The residence was among the earliest brick structures in Alabama. Inherited by his son, William Pope, the mansion was sold in 1848 to Dr. Charles Hays Patton, who commissioned George Steele to add the handsome classical revival portico. Nearby during the Civil War, Federal forces built an earthen breastwork with lumber taken from the Georgia Slave Graveyard to defend approaches to the city.

Pope sold the two acres of the cemetery to the city of Huntsville on September 14, 1822.[30] This was due to an ordinance passed by the City Council that required separate burial places for blacks and whites. Possibly another incentive for purchasing the new cemetery had to do with this new rule. City officials continued to use it for burials of blacks.

Georgia Cemetery became a focal point for the black community, possibly because it was the only place in Huntsville they could claim as their own. The Huntsville African Baptist Church, which later became Saint Bartley Primitive Baptist Church, traces its beginning back to 1820, when slaves met under the dogwood trees in the cemetery to hear God's word delivered by their first pastor, Elder William Harris.[31] In 1808, slaves

[30] Leroy Pope, *Southern Advocate*, Huntsville, June 21, 1844.
[31] Ginger Underwood, *Alabama: Free People of Color*, (Tuscaloosa: University Press of Alabama, 2005), 53.

slipped away at night to go to the cemetery and worship with Elder Harris. However, in 1820, it officially was established as a church in the cemetery under the name of the Huntsville African Baptist Church, a possible offshoot of a similar church in Savannah, Georgia, where Elder Harris had preached when he left the plantation as a free slave.

In 1833, a law was enacted that forbade slaves from gathering unless a white man was present who could prevent slaves from discussing or planning freedom. Sermons were even censored for the same reason. Many of Huntsville's older black residents remember the oral histories that were handed down about slaves meeting in the cemetery late at night, preaching in whispers so they would not be overheard. Others remember stories about black preachers delivering sermons in a singsong fashion that the white masters would not be able to understand.

After the war, the area known as Georgia became a thriving community. Many of the newly freed slaves made it their home and opened small businesses. The church and the cemetery played a large role in the community's religious and social life, a fact the city must have realized when its appropriated money to build gates to the cemetery.

In 1870, the city purchased land for another black cemetery, which would become known as Glenwood. Many have speculated as to why the city purchased another cemetery. The answer is obvious when one considers the relatively small size of Georgia Cemetery, the average population in Huntsville, and the prevailing death rate. Georgia Cemetery, with almost two thousand graves, if not full, was close to it. Another possible reason related to the advancement of emancipated black members and freed slaves of the black community, many of whom had no desire to be buried in what was known as a slave cemetery.

Even with the purchase of Glenwood, evidence and oral histories suggest that burials continued to take place in Georgia. Construction work at the Georgia site in recent years has unearthed graves containing clothing and casket styles that clearly indicate that Georgia Cemetery was used for burials after 1900. Other evidence can be found in the Madison County Deed Book 2, page 275, which contains the description of the sale of land known as Longwood plantation, which came into the sole ownership of Harry M. Rhett on November 7, 1903. This land adjoined

Georgia Cemetery, and in the surveyor's report, it is referred to as being on "the south boundary of the African Cemetery."[32]

The cemetery is also pictured in the original 1902 Quigley map of Huntsville. The fragile book that contains this map clearly shows the Georgia Cemetery identified simply as Colored Cemetery.

The graveyard began a gradual decay. Tombstones were no longer replaced, and it became overgrown, with the city seemingly taking no interest in maintaining it. Harry Rhett, who owned the adjacent land, took personal interest in the cemetery, often sending his employees to cut weeds and maintain the grounds. Rhett was also instrumental in the movement to build a new hospital.

The original hospital was in a house on Gallatin Street that had originally been an infamous bordello. Its Madame, Mollie Teal, had bequeathed the house to the city in her will, with the stipulation that it be used as a hospital. No doubt the hospital officials, besides needing larger facilities, were also anxious to rid themselves of the house's reputation. On June 30, 1925, Harry and Louise Rhett deeded the tract of land bordering the cemetery to the city for the construction of Huntsville Hospital. Probably fearing for the future of the cemetery, Rhett stipulated in the deed that the gift was contingent upon the hospital acquiring the cemetery next to it and maintaining it. Rhett, realizing that good intentions often have short memories, also stipulated in the deed that, if the parties failed to live up to the agreement, the land would revert to him or his heirs.

Less than three weeks later, on July 19, 1925, the city of Huntsville deeded the cemetery to the Huntsville Hospital. Strangely, and for reasons unknown, the deed omitted all mention of a cemetery and even contained the sentence, "It is seized in fee thereof and that the same are free from encumbrances."[33] The new hospital was erected adjacent to the Georgia Cemetery and, for some period of time, the cemetery was largely ignored. Remaining headstones gradually disappeared or were moved off, and Georgia Cemetery appeared to be just another vacant field. The swampy nature of the area was corrected in the 1950s when proper drainage was installed, making the land attractive to investors. A city parking garage

---

[32] Leslie Jeffreys, "The Georgia Cemetery," Folklore Family, Rootsweb.ancestry.com, April 5, 2001.

[33] Ibid.

for the hospital was later built on part of the cemetery, and the rest of it disappeared under slabs of concrete as the city tried to keep up with the growing medical needs. For all intents and purposes, it was as if the Georgia Cemetery never existed.

Were all the bodies moved? We know they were still there on June 30, 1925, or Harry Rhett would have had no reason to be concerned about the upkeep of the cemetery. A careful search of the records shows no mention of any removals. In all likelihood, city officials in 1925 simply decided that public needs clearly outweighed a cemetery that had not been used for fifteen or twenty years.

On September 3, 1818, the Huntsville City Commissioners purchased two acres of land from LeRoy Pope for a burying ground for slaves. This cemetery was located within the northeast quarter of Section 1, Township 4, Range 1 West of the Base Meridian. It was affectionately known as "Georgia" within the black community. The cemetery continued to be used from 1818 until 1870, when Glenwood Cemetery was designated as the city's burial ground for African Americans. No known records have survived. The marker was erected by Alabama Historical Association.

Site of the Huntsville Slave Cemetery marker, looking across Madison Street toward the marker.

The building is part of the Huntsville Hospital complex.

(Picture and site by Rev. Isaiah Robinson, October 20, 2020)

The Georgia Slave Graveyard marker
(Picture by Rev. Isaiah Robinson, October 20, 2020)

The Glenwood Cemetery
(Picture by Rev. Isaiah Robinson, October 20, 2020)

Glenwood Cemetery replaced the original slave cemetery, known as "Georgia," which had been established in 1818 and was located north of the present Huntsville Hospital. Glenwood Cemetery was established in 1870 by the City of Huntsville, following the purchase of ten acres from the Benjamin W. Blake estate, originally a part of the John Brahan Plantation. Additional land was added in 1875, from the W.W. Darwin family, resulting in the current configuration.

Distinguished African Americans buried here include veterans of America's wars, beginning with the Civil War; former slaves; accomplished artisans; professionals in many fields; clergymen, educators, entrepreneurs, and politicians; and other leaders.

Glenwood Cemetery is located at the intersection of Hall Avenue NW and Derrick Avenue NW and the intersection of Madison Street and Saint Clair Avenue, Huntsville, Alabama. On September 3, 1818, Leroy Pope sold two acres to the city of Huntsville for seventy-five dollars for use as a city burial ground. He sold an additional two acres, which would become Maple Hill Cemetery, at which point the original two acres was designated as a slave graveyard and was known as the Old Georgia Graveyard. In 1870, the city moved the cemetery to ten acres between Holmes and Clinton Avenue from land originally part of the John Brahan Plantation, and in 1875, additional land from the W.W. Darwin family was added to Glenwood.

There were no burial records; it is unknown how many bodies were moved to the new cemetery, Glenwood, and how many remained. Old Georgia was located where the parking garage for Huntsville Hospital is today. The exact number of graves in Glenwood is unknown but is estimated to be up to ten thousand, including over a thousand belonging to slaves, as well as prominent members of Huntsville's African American community. Among them are Dr. Burgess Scruggs, the first African American physician in Alabama, and Charles Hendley Jr., editor of the influential *Huntsville Gazette*.[34]

Maple Hill Cemetery
Located at the southeast corner of Wells Avenue and Maple Hill Road.

Maple Hill Cemetery was established in 1822 from land sold to the city of Huntsville by Leroy Pope. The cemetery sprawls out over seventy-six acres and is brimming with Huntsville and Alabama history. Regarded as the oldest continually used cemetery in Alabama, Maple Hill boasts somewhere between eighty thousand and a hundred thousand burials. Among the graves lie five Alabama governors, five Civil War Union officers, around two hundred unknown Confederate soldiers, the parents of actress Tallulah Bankhead, "Father of Huntsville" Leroy Pope, and artist Maria Howard Weeden.

[34] Kelly Kazek, "Are there 9,000 Unmarked Graves in Huntsville Slave Cemetery?" AL.com, July 29, 2015.

The St. Bartley Primitive Baptist Church
1872–1965

*(Photo courtesy of the book King Cotton to Space Capital,
1965, from Huntsville Public Library Special Collections)*

The rebuilt St. Bartley's was located on what is now Williams Street. There's a marker at the spot where the church stood until 1965, when it was torn down for urban renewal. Elder Bartley Harris led the church for many years and was known as the pastor who held huge baptisms at the Big Spring at the bottom of the hill from the church. It is said that he baptized as many as three hundred in one day.

This was an annual event, and the baptisms were held on the second Sunday in May of each year. So many people attended the service that, one time, the foot bridge over the Spring branched collapsed with the crowd.

Saint Bartley's baptism was almost a social event, with people coming in their Sunday Best and other churches closing on that Sunday because everyone would be gone to the Big Brick.[35]

The women candidates for baptism wore long white robes and white

---

[35] *The Huntsville Journal*, Huntsville, Alabama, May 24, 1893.

bandannas. They had a worship service at the church first. Then they marched by two out of the church down the hill to the Big Spring Branch. As they came, they sang improvised hymns. The technical term for it is wording it out. They were followed by the congregation singing "Swing Low, Sweet Chariot." Stopping at the edge of the water, they waited in exultation as the minister and his assistant in long black frock coats descended to the middle of the stream near the footbridge.

Loud prayers and invocation of the Holy Spirit were shouted over the waters. The candidates were led to the water one by one. After the baptisms, the crowd sung a hymn and gradually receded, satisfied they had witnessed a great event at the Big Spring. The area of the Big Spring used for baptizing is today located between the Central Bank and First Alabama Bank buildings in downtown Huntsville.

On May 18, 1893, St. Bartley held a baptizing event at the Big Spring Branch on Sunday. Many new members were baptized by immersion. Elder William Gaston helped to officiate.[36]

The Big Spring is a large, underground karst spring. Hearing of the abundant water source and plentiful big game, John Hunt, Huntsville's founder, sought out the spring and settled near it in 1805 on the bluff above, which later became the site of the First National Bank of Huntsville. Isaac and Joseph Criner had previously reached the Big Spring and considered settlement but, due to the presence of bears and mosquitoes, left to settle New Market instead. During the nineteenth century and the first half of the twentieth century, the spring was Huntsville's water source, due to its massive flow.

The Big Spring is the largest limestone spring in North Alabama, with its usual flow between 7 and 20 million US gallons (76,000 m³) per day, depending on the time of the year. Big Spring Park is named for the spring so named by the indigenous Cherokee and Chickasaw.[37]

---

[36] Ibid., May 24, 1893.
[37] Ibid.

Baptism was a yearly event for St. Bartley, held on the second Sunday in May. It was almost a "social event," as many would come in their "Sunday Best" and other churches would cancel their services and attend service at the "Big Brick" that Sunday. The women candidates for baptism wore long white robes and white bandannas. At the conclusion of worship service, they would walk down the hill to the Big Spring Branch singing congregational hymns (improvised hymns known as wording it out).[38] Stopping at the edge of the water, they waited in exultation as the minister and his assistant in long black frock coats descended to the middle of the stream near the footbridge. Loud prayers and invocation of the Holy Spirit were over the waters. The candidates were led to the water one by one. After baptism, they would sing a hymn, satisfied that they had witnessed a great event at the Big Spring. There was a lot of shouting and praising God going on throughout the service.

[38] Ibid.

Elder Bartley Harris
The portrait of Saint Bartley Harris is a late nineteenth-
century watercolor portrait by Maria Howard
Weeden, an artist from Huntsville, Alabama.
(photo courtesy of Weeden House Museum)

Elder Bartley Harris, Sr., was the second pastor of Saint Bartley Primitive Baptist Church. As with Elder William Harris, Elder Bartley Harris was the grandson of the church founder Elder William Harris. According to records from the twenty-first annual session of the Indian Creek Primitive Baptist Association held in Madison, Alabama, Elder Bartley Harris was still the pastor of the Saint Bartley Primitive Baptist Church in 1891.[39] He moved the church from the Georgia Graveyard in 1872 to the Oak Avenue location, and the church was renamed to honor him. Once a person notices the original cornerstone, they will see that it reads "St. Bartley's." It is not known when the apostrophe was dropped or removed from the church name.

Elder Bartley Harris was well loved by the white and black community. Both black and white referred to him as Uncle Bartley Harris. The famous old hard-shell Baptist preacher, a remarkable character, left a lasting impression on the religious life of the black people of Huntsville. "Uncle Bartley Harris" was a landmark as firmly fixed in the lives of the older black people as the Big Spring, the courthouse, or the centuries-old oak

---

[39] Minutes of the Indian Creek Primitive Baptist Association, September 1891.

tree on Adams Avenue. (This tree has been cut down as of the writing of this manuscript.) The original cornerstone of the church read, "Erected AD 1872," and underneath, "St. Bartley's."[40]

There had been many eminent divines and many forceful preachers, but never before had one been canonized by the loyalty of his flock, and in his own lifetime at that. It was a simple but significant dedication and was indicative of a people's devotion to their pastor. Elder Bartley Harris was known among the members as Father Bartley Harris, and he'd served pastor of the Saint Bartley Primitive Baptist Church for fifty years. He received and baptized over four thousand members. He was assisted in later years by Elder William Gaston, an associate minister of St. Bartley. He was almost one hundred years of age when he died. He was a powerful, moving preacher. He baptized until he was so old he could not hold the candidates in the water, so he got some of the younger brothers, like Elder Gaston, to hold them, and he lay his hand on them and said, "I baptize you in the name of the Father, the Son, and the Holy Ghost."

It is said that, when he came to Huntsville, he worked as a free man for Daniel Harris, who had a large plantation near Huntsville in the Harvest area. When Daniel Harris's slaves were divided, he gave Bartley Harris to his daughter, Martha Jinny. Bartley married Martha Jinny and had seventeen children; the oldest boy was named Bartley Harris Jr.[41]

Elder Bartley Harris baptized over four thousand members into the Primitive Baptist faith, and it is said he made a picturesque and commanding figure as he stood in the waters of the Big Spring, his tall figure enveloped in a long linen duster and his head bound with a white turban. Elder Harris was six feet tall and stood very erect in his youth, but as the years bore down upon him, he grew stooped and bent. He was born brown skinned and wore a close-cropped gray beard. He had a powerful voice, and he swayed his emotional audiences with his eloquence and fervor.

On a Sunday, while all the Christian world was singing praises to Him that is risen, all that was mortal of Elder Bartley Harris passed quietly from his earthly labors to the great beyond. As a faithful worker in the Lord's vineyard, he stood preeminent. Loved, honored, and respected by

---

[40] Minutes of the Historic Ministry of the Saint Bartley Primitive Baptist Church, 1967.
[41] Ibid.

all, he became the counselor, friend, and father to the poor and needy. Ever charitable, ever anxious and willing to point the way of salvation to those out of the fold, he was revered by all who knew him. He fellowshipped closely with William Hooper Councill an ex-slave who founded and pastored the St. John AME Church in Huntsville.

The Burning of St. Bartley Church

(Pictures courtesy of The Huntsville Journal, April 10, 1896, Huntsville Public Library Special Collections)

As reported in *The Huntsville Gazette* on November 26, 1887, "The roof and interior of St. Bartley Primitive Baptist Church was destroyed by fire last Sunday. The fire, which was discovered in the southwest corner of the building about eleven o'clock is supposed to have originated from a defective flue. The Fire and the Hook and Ladder companies were early on the scene and through their heroic efforts quelled the flames and saved the adjourning houses. Now with the present structure burned, the church was rebuilt with the assistance from the United States government which sent an additional $400 to start the church."[42]

And in *The Huntsville Journal* in April 1896, it was reported, "Last Sunday, while all the Christian world were singing praises to Him [Christ] that is risen, after preaching a dynamic heavenly sermon, all that was mortal of Elder Bartley Harris passed quietly from his earthly labors to the great beyond." He died on April 2, 1896,[43] according to The Huntsville Gazette.

---

[42] *The Huntsville Gazette*, Saturday, November 26, 1887.
[43] *The Huntsville Journal*, Friday, April 10, 1896.

As a faithful worker in the Lord's vineyard, he stood preeminent. Loved, honored, and respected by all, he became the counselor, friend, and father to the poor and needy. Ever charitable, ever anxious and willing to point the way of salvation to those out of the fold, he was revered by all who knew him.

The funeral service was attended at the St. Bartley Primitive Baptist Church, where he pastored, that Monday and was one of the most impressive ever witnessed in Huntsville. The eulogy was performed by Elder Felix Jordan, the third pastor of St. Bartley. The pathetic scene at the Georgia Graveyard cemetery where he was buried and where the last rites were being performed, evidenced the love and devotion people held for him.

Elder Bartley Harris's funeral was the greatest event ever seen in Huntsville at that time, with thousands of people attending. They crowded around the hearse and moved and marched in a solid mass from St. Bartley Church to the last resting place of their beloved old saint. He was later supposedly buried in the Glenwood Cemetery when the Georgia Graveyard was closed. His portrait was painted by famous local artist Maria Howard Weeden. His picture appeared on the front cover of *Southern Woman's Magazine*, August 1916.[44]

ELDER BARTLEY HARRIS, SR,

*Pastor Bartley Harris Sr., born 1800 in
Virginia, died April 2, 1896.
(Photo courtesy Weeden House Museum)*

---

[44] Elizabeth Price, "St. Bartley," *Southern Woman's Magazine*, August 1916.

Maria Howard Weeden (July 6, 1846–April 12, 1905), who signed her work and published as Howard Weeden, was an American artist and poet based in Huntsville, Alabama. After the American Civil War, she began to sell works she painted, which included portraits of many African American freedmen and freedwomen, including the painting of Elder Bartley Harris. As a white woman living in the postbellum South, Weeden's choice to paint Saint Bartley and other African American individuals was unique.

Many of the individuals she painted remain unnamed, as they were freedmen and women who worked for her family or neighboring families in positions such as cooks and gardeners after the Civil War, but Saint Bartley is an exception.

Bartley Harris was a prominent and influential public figure for both African Americans and whites in late nineteenth-century Huntsville. He was known for his massive baptisms in Huntsville's "Big Spring" and for his hiding of local Confederates' valuables in his church during the Civil War. He was an instrumental figure in the early history of the Huntsville African Baptist Church (he served as its second pastor), which survives today as Saint Bartley Primitive Baptist Church, Alabama's oldest African American congregation. Harris's local prominence may be one of the reasons Hugh Walker, in his 1962 newspaper article "Shadows on the Wall: Howard Who Was a Girl," labeled Weeden's portrait of Saint Bartley Harris one of her most well-known.[45]

The portrait of Saint Bartley Harris is unique, in that it was not one of Weeden's many portraits of African Americans included in her illustrated volumes of poetry, four of which were published between 1898 and 1904. Her portrait of St. Bartley Harris, in fact, had an unusually broad and cosmopolitan audience; it was one of only seven of her paintings exhibited in Berlin, Germany, in 1896, where it was reportedly well received. This exhibition was facilitated by Weeden's Nashville friend Elizabeth Price, who played an instrumental role in promoting and disseminating Weeden's works at home and abroad. Elizabeth Price showed Weeden's painting of Saint Bartley Harris, along with six other portraits, to Edward Schulte, a gallery owner in Berlin, after which he offered to display her paintings.

---

[45] Frances C. Roberts and Sarah Huff Fisk, *Shadows on the Wall: The Life and Works of Howard Weeden* (Northport, AL: Colonial Press, 1962) 8, 9, 12, 13, 15, 19, 20, 21, 22, 131. LCCN 63-1883.

Today, Weeden's portrait of St. Bartley hangs in her historic home, which has been converted to the Weeden House Museum in the Twickenham Historic District of Huntsville, Alabama.[46]

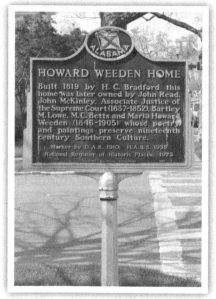

---

[46] Hugh Walker, "Shadows on the Wall: Howard Who Was a Girl," *Nashville Tennessean* 57, no. 221 (December 9, 1962), 13, Gannett Co., Inc. via ProQuest Historical Newspapers.

THE PEOPLE AND EVENTS
OF THE NEW ERA

It became apparent that the number of free persons of color grew within Huntsville. Obviously, the free Negro population was not leaving, and emancipations, perhaps of kinship ties, continued even after restrictive laws were enacted. And of course, free parents would want their children to remain with their family if the atmosphere was indulgent about the legal limitations.

No matter the penalties and restrictions, by 1860, the population of free people in the United States was 260,000 in number. Once at liberty, perhaps the greatest fear for a newly freed person of color was the possibility of being stolen and re-enslaved. Kidnapping in some states had become so blatant that the crime became a capital offense. For instance, in Delaware the punishment for kidnapping a black person was thirty-nine lashes and both ears nailed to the pillory for an hour and then cut off. Although black and white people often lived side by side, the separation was unyielding. "We reside among you and yet are strangers; natives, and yet not citizens; surrounded by the freest people and most republican institutions in the world, and yet enjoying none of the immunities of freedom ... Though we are not slaves, we are not free."[47]

Most free people of color lived in town clustered around other modest

---

[47] *The Huntsville Journal*, May 20, 1893.

black and white and poor and working-class people but still convenient to upper-class households who needed their services. Housing probably was not good for any of these families and restricted to small areas in back alleys, above stores, and in dank cellars or unoccupied sheds and lean-tos. Like most of their white neighbors, the lives of free blacks centered on work, family, and church. Putting food on the table and clothing on their backs required most of their time.

Additionally, they also might fish at nearby Pinhook Creek or hunt with traps in the woods at the edge of town. (It was against the law for blacks to have weapons.) Free people of color would never expect to sit with whites at a public gathering, much less enter the Opera House, the local epitome of white culture. If the law was strictly adhered to, taverns, restaurants, and hotels were also off limits. While free blacks had little time for entertainment, they might occasionally gather at a horse race or cock fight. Political figures of the day held frequent barbeques, and black people were almost certainly involved. At the very least, they cooked, served, and cleaned. Most blacks worshipped at the Huntsville African Baptist Church, which later was renamed Saint Bartley Primitive Baptist Church, on Oak Street.

Unlike the slave, a free person of color was his own master, possessing the right to his own labor, his own occupation, and his own hours. In Alabama, he had the right of marriage without asking permission unless the intended spouse was still a slave; the master then had to agree. Many Negroes were accustomed to "jumping backward over the broom" as part of the ceremony to see which one of the couples would be the boss. But the words of the ceremony often mentioned the couple would be married "as long as distance did not separate us," for instance, if the slave owner moved away.

The respect for the sanctity and legality of marriage led freedman Charles Sampson, in 1822, to make the trip into town from Madison Station for a marriage license for himself and Irene Smith. Their daughter, Matilda, also had a license for her marriage to Nelson Earls in 1855.

The 1805 and 183,3 marriage codes allowed officials to "solemnize the rites of matrimony between any free persons" who presented a license. By 1852 the Code of Alabama contained a significant change.[48]

Article 1946 noted that "marriage may be solemnized between free white persons, or between free persons of color, by any licensed minister" while article 1956 added, "Any person solemnizing the rites of matrimony, with the knowledge that … one of the parties is a Negro [slave or free] and the other a white person is guilty of a misdemeanor."[49] A mother could now enjoy the freedom to name her baby to her liking.

Southerners were proud to note they encouraged blacks to attend church. Religious instruction by slave owners served to teach slaves the white views of morality and obedience. Some allowed slaves to attend their master's church, sitting in the back pews or the balcony. The message often came from Ephesians 6:5: "Servants be obedient to them that are your masters." Perhaps less seldom heard was Colossians 4:1: "Masters, be just and fair to your slaves. Remember that you also have a Master in heaven" (NKJV).

The restrictions placed on their church services (one observer, Presbyterian minister Charles Colcock Jones noted in 1832) as the results of "religious persecution, secrecy and nocturnal meetings" led to more secrecy in old fields and plantations. This attitude provided further validation for those who argued that religious instruction and behavior of blacks be constantly supervised. Observation by white men must, by law, accompany any religious service with more than five or six members. Even in these circumstances, almost everyone felt strong ties to their religious beliefs. As among our people generally, the Church is the Alpha and Omega of all things. Religion became the hub of many blacks' social life, even as they were aware that, by law, a white person would be present at the majority of gatherings.

Elder Bartley Harris continued to preach "election of grace." Instead of seventy-six missionary members, there are thousands of Primitive Baptists. The Rev. W. H. Gaston, who served with the Union Army, now was the

---

[48] James E. Bates, *Alabama: Free People of Color* (Tuscaloosa: University of Alabama Press, April 10, 2006), 95–98.
[49] William Warren Rogers, Robert David Ward, Leah Rawls Atkins, and Wayne Flynn, *Alabama: The History of the Deep South State* (Tuscaloosa: The University of Alabama Press, 1994), 110–112.

leading educator among the congregation at St. Bartley. In 1821, Gaston accompanied Elder William Harris to become a member of the Flint River Association, with seventy-six members. Rev. Gaston established a school in Huntsville under the auspices of St. Bartley.[50]

The Baptists organized the first churches in the Huntsville area three years before the town was incorporated. Flint River Primitive Baptist Church was organized in October 1808, while Enon Baptist, which would become First Baptist Huntsville, came into being on June 3, 1809. First Baptist showed evidence of a limited slave ministry from its first year of operation. The church received its first recorded slave members when Ben and Peg Camady joined the church two days before its first anniversary.

The church's slave population grew slowly until 1815 and greatly picked up momentum in the 1820s. Whereas eighteen slaves had passed through First Baptist's doors from its foundation until 1820, the church saw more than fifty new slaves pass through during the 1820s. Of the seventy slaves who came to First Baptist in its first twenty years, only twenty went elsewhere, giving the church nearly fifty slave members by 1830. The most active year during that decade was 1827, when twenty-five slaves from eleven families joined the church. Eleven of those slaves joined on April 1, all by experience of salvation and baptism. It's likely that the church had experienced revival shortly before the April service, and the revival may have been conducted outside the church, since the minutes make no mention of special services.

While a new life was going on in the black church, the white churches were continuing to manifest themselves with certain issues. The Enon Church was organized on the bank of the Flint River on June 3, 1809. It was first named West Fork Baptist Church of Flint River.

The church started in Madison County when it was part of the Mississippi Territory ten years before Alabama became a state. Eventually the name was changed to First Baptist Church Governors Drive on August 9, 1893. On October 23, 1823, the Baptist State Convention of Alabama was organized at the Salem church in Greensboro, Alabama. The Enon Church was a member of the Flint River Association but left the Flint River Association and formed the Liberty Baptist Association in 1838. That association, which met in its first annual association on November 2–3,

---

[50] Boothe, *The Cyclopedia of Colored Baptist in Alabama*, 1845.

1838, baptized twelve white members and twenty-two black members. The Southern Baptist Convention was organized in Augusta, Georgia, on May 8, 1845. The reason for the organizing was a desire to separate from the American Baptist Home Mission Society, which made a policy that no slaveholder could be appointed a missionary. The Enon Church was the only Baptist church of missionary persuasion in the city of Huntsville. The Enon Church occupied the Bell Tower Building at the corner of Clinton and Gallatin Street until it moved to Governors Drive in 1893.[51]

In 1872, the St. Bartley Primitive Baptist Church was relocated to Oak Avenue, near Gallatin Street, near Fountain Row (also known as Henry Street) on the southwest side of Huntsville. It was a gray brick building with Gothic windows of ornamental glass and was the largest Negro church in Alabama and became known as the "Big Brick."[52]

Because of Elder Harris's relationship with the white community and the service he provided to them when the Union Soldiers were there, many of them provided funds for the purchase of materials for the new church. There were those who brought the Gothic windows and ornamental glass. Much of the interior was provided by free slaves and whites. Many of them joined in building the structure. The building was outstanding for that time. The church was burned in 1886, and members held worship services in the Rust Normal School located on Franklin Street, from 1886 to 1887. Elder Bartley Harris wrote to the *Huntsville Gazette* on December 12, 1887, an appeal for assistance in rebuilding St. Bartley, which had caught fire in the rear of the church. The *Gazette* article regarding the fire, reported:[53]

> The roof and interior of St. Bartley Primitive Baptist Church was destroyed by fire last Sunday, the fire, which was discovered in the southwest corner of the building about 11 pm is supposed to have originated from a defective flue. The Fire and the Hook and Ladder companies were early on the scene and through their heroic efforts quelled the flames and saved the adjoining frame houses.

[51] Ibid., 45–49.
[52] Ibid., 21–24.
[53] *Huntsville Gazette*, December 12, 1887.

Harris's letter read:

Dear Editor Sir:

Many of our brethren and friends are anxious to know what steps will be taken and when we shall begin to repair our church was burned on November 20, 1887. Please allow me to say that the contract was let out today to Mr. J. M. Hutchens at the lowest bid made $1441.50, half to be paid April 1, 1888, when work is complete and the rest in twelve months with interest. We have on hand in cash, $265.45 collected since the burning, $56.75 subscribed to be given in on the last Sabbath in January 1988 by our brethren, sisters, and friends, white and colored.

There are a great many others who guarantee to meet us at said times with cash, so that we hope to have $500.00 by the middle of February 1888. We hereby tender our sincere thanks to the friend who have liberally assisted us to the present.

While we have not had occasion to call on our northern brethren before for help, we beg leave to state, that we are the only sect. South, that we know, which has not been assisted by a sect of the same creed from the North. We hope our Northern brethren will now extend a helping hand.

Work has begun, and we hope to see the cove on so that we can commence services at the church in three or four weeks. Friends are cordially solicited, now, to aid in whatever sums of money and ways they feel to assist us.

Respectfully,
Elder Bartley Harris, Pastor; Elder William Gaston, Clerk; Huntsville Primitive Baptist Church— Huntsville, Ala., December 12, 1887.[54]

---

[54] *Huntsville Gazette*, November 1887.

St. Bartley was eventually rebuilt with the assistance of brethren, sisters, friends, and the help of the United States government, who sent $400 to get construction started.

Elder William Gaston
1935–1996

William Gaston joined the Huntsville African Baptist Church under its founder Elder William Harris after the Civil War. Gaston was sergeant major of the 12th United States Colored Troops. After the war, he came home and taught school and prosecuted pension claims. He was a faithful and dedicated member under Elder William Harris and assisted him with many aspects of the church and association. He served faithfully also under Elder Bartley Harris, the second pastor, as clerk of the church for over thirty years. He served as an alderman for two terms from the fourth ward in the city of Huntsville. He voluntarily retired due to sickness.

In 1868, he received his mustered-out money for serving in the Union Army. He was one of the esteemed members of the Indian Creek Primitive Baptist Association, being one of its founders in 1871, and served as clerk for many years. He was a member of the Trustee Board of the association. In 1866, St. Bartley Primitive Baptist Church was providing education for black children, with the school, known as the Huntsville Graded and Industrial School, located in St. Bartley Church and Gaston as its first principal and teacher. He also served as associate minister of St. Bartley.[55]

Elder Gaston was the son of Abram Athborn and Roda Gaston, born in Huntsville, Alabama in 1835. His wife was Jane Gaston. They had three children, Cornelius, Matilda, and Annah. His siblings were Samuel Miller, Geston, Ann, and Kimball.[56]

A mass meeting of colored citizens was held in 1891, and results were forthcoming. Trustees for a school were elected, including H. C. Binford, J. B. Carter, W. H. Gaston, J. F. Humphrey, Sidney Pentecost, Emanual McCalley, and Charles Moore.

These trustees secured a one-acre lot from Nicholas Davis in the Davis

---

[55] Boothe, *Cyclopedia*, 56–60.

[56] William Gaston, a black educator and minister, served as assistant pastor of Saint Bartley Primitive Baptist Church for thirty-five years.

Grove between Pearl and Pump Streets and were rewarded later in 1892 by seeing the city award a contract to C. E. Hutchens for a two-story frame school building, the first publicly owned building in Huntsville's public school history for black students. The building was dedicated on October 15, 1894, and served until 1927, when a brick building replaced the frame structure and became known as William H. Councill school (Record II).[57]

The historic marker for William Hooper Councill High School reads, "The first public school for African Americans in the city of Huntsville was named for the founder of the Alabama A&M University. The site, selected by a committee headed by the Rev. W. E. Gaston, was donated by the Davis-Lowe family. Founded in 1867 in the basement of Lakeside Methodist Episcopal Church on Jefferson Street, the school was moved to a frame building on this site in 1892. The first diplomas were granted in 1912. A brick structure replaced the original building in 1927. The school was closed due to integration, graduating its last class in 1966."[58]

Rev. William Gaston officiated in the immersion baptism of many new colored church members in the Big Spring on Sunday, May 18, 1893.[59]

Elder Gaston died in 1896, and his funeral was held Wednesday at 2:00 p.m. on February 10, 1896, at the St. Bartley Primitive Baptist Church, with Elders Elias Patton, J. J. Smith, B. I. Chapman, and Felix Jordan officiating. The pallbearers were Elders Braziel and R. L. Laws; Deacons John Seay and C. H. Ware; and Reverends G. W. Blankenship, Richard Burns, Charlie Sawyer, and Henry Johnson. He was buried in Glenwood Cemetery.[60]

---

[57] James Record, "Record II—A Dream Come True: The Story of Madison County and Incidentally of Alabama and the United States" volume II (1978), 78, 358.

[58] Frank Alex Luttrell, III, ed., *Historical Markers of Madison County, Alabama* (2001), 74, 101.

[59] Raneé G. Pruitt, ed., *Eden of the South: A Chronology of Huntsville, Alabama, 1805–2005* (2005), 86.

[60] Huntsville Directory Company, City Directory—Huntsville City Directory 1896–1897, 93.

**President Ulysses Grant,
eighteenth president of the United States**

*Picture courtesy of St. Bartley Primitive Baptist
Church Historical Ministry Minutes, 34)*

Hiram Ulysses Grant (April 27, 1822–July 23, 1885) was an American soldier and politician who served as the eighteenth president of the United States from 1869 to 1877. Before his presidency, Grant led the Union Army in winning the American Civil War.

A war hero but a reluctant politician, Grant was unanimously nominated by the Republican Party and was elected president in 1868. As president, Grant stabilized the postwar national economy, created the Department of Justice, and prosecuted the Ku Klux Klan.[61]

He appointed African Americans and Jewish Americans to prominent federal offices. In 1871, he created the first Civil Service Commission. The Liberal Republicans and Democrats united behind Grant's opponent in the presidential election of 1872, but Grant was handily reelected. Grant used the reconstruction acts, which had been passed over Johnson's veto, to enforce civil rights for African freedmen. Grant's presidential accomplishments included the Alabama Claims settlement, protection of blacks and Indians, and the first Civil Service Commission. Among these,

---

[61] Louis Coolidge, Ulysses S. Grant (Boston & New York: Houghton Mifflin Co., 1917), scholarly review doi:10.14296/RiH/2014/2270. Picture courtesy of Mathew B. Brady (c. 1822 – January 15, 1896). (Library of Congress domain)

the Alabama Claims related to depredations caused to the Union by the Confederate was the most pressing diplomatic problem in 1869.[62]

The original church building of the Huntsville African Baptist Church (St. Bartley) was destroyed by fire during the Union occupation after the Civil War and was rebuilt in 1872 by Elder Bartley Harris with money appropriated by President Grant and the United States Congress. People or organizations who suffered financial losses during the conflict and who could prove they were not sympathetic to the Confederacy were entitled to compensation from the Federal government. President Ulysses S. Grant signed the appropriation papers authorizing the transfer of those funds. After the war, President Grant heard of the soldiers' actions and realized their action were wrong, so he appropriated money for rebuilding the church.[63]

The Reconstruction period was a time of increased political activity in Alabama's black community after enfranchisement.

Given their general emphasis on liberation theology and a holistic view of the church's role in the community, it's not surprising that black Baptist ministers were among the political leaders and office holders during this period. In some cases, their churches provided a base for political activities.

The outcome of the American Civil War ended slavery in Alabama. The Thirteenth Amendment permanently abolished slavery in the United States in 1865. Alabama freed people welcomed emancipation but endured continuing hardships because of the prevailing and pervasive racial prejudices of the state's white inhabitants. Alabama's antebellum-era slave codes were replaced by postbellum social and legal system of separating citizens on the basis of race that remained intact through the mid-twentieth century. The racist theology that had once excused the actions of the state's slaveholders survived the Civil War and emancipation and carried over into the postbellum era to support an array of Jim Crow laws that trampled on the civil liberties of African Americans until they were overturned during the civil rights movement. Elder Bartley Harris, the pastor of St. Bartley Primitive Baptist Church, preached that man is saved by grace alone with his faith in Jesus Christ. He led the church into

[62] Charles W. Calhoun, *The Presidency of Ulysses S. Grant* (Lawrence: University Press of Kansas), ISBN 978-0-7006-2484-3, 48–56.
[63] Ibid., 52.

the Primitive Baptist fold as they upheld their belief in salvation by the grace of God and that scripture alone should guide one's faith and life. In keeping with this firm belief in scripture, they believed that all men are equal in the eyes of God: "There is neither Jew nor Greek, there is neither slave nor free there is neither male or female; for you are all one in Christ Jesus" (Galatians 3:28 NKJV).

During this period of time, the St. Bartley Primitive Baptist Church, under the leadership of Elder Bartley Harris as pastor, led the way for many black to achieve important positions in the community.

Elder William Gaston; Elder Daniel Brandon, alderman; C. C. Moore, first black postman; Burgess E. Scruggs, Huntsville's first African American physician; and Charles Hendley, Jr., editor of the *Huntsville Gazette* were all affiliated with St. Bartley Church and held many positions in the community.

With St. Bartley Primitive Baptist Church leading the way as the first black church in Alabama, other churches began and associated with St. Bartley and Elder Harris in Huntsville.

Church Street Cumberland Presbyterian Church was established in 1874 as the first black Cumberland Presbyterian church in the nation and was one of the first in Huntsville, Alabama. The reverend Hampton Jones served as its first pastor from 1874 to 1800.[64]

William Hooper Councill, educator and race leader, was born into slavery in Fayetteville, North Carolina, on July 12, 1849. His parents were both slaves on the Councill plantation. When William was five, his father escaped to Canada and tried unsuccessfully to obtain freedom for his family. In 1857, William, his mother, and his brother Cicero were sold at the Richmond slave market to a trader, who in turn sold them on to a planter in Alabama. His two other brothers were sold separately. When Union troops occupied Chattanooga, Tennessee, during the Civil War, Councill and his family escaped through Union lines to the North. He returned to Alabama in 1865 to attend a school for freedmen that had been started by Quakers in Stevenson, Alabama. This would be Councill's only formal schooling. He worked and studied for three years before graduating in 1867.[65]

---

[64] Boothe, *Cyclopedia*, 61–62.
[65] Ibid., 1,870–72

For several years, Councill worked as a teacher in the black public schools in Alabama while moonlighting as a porter in hotels and restaurants. In 1869, at the age of twenty-two, he opened Lincoln School in Huntsville for black children in the region. In addition to his teaching duties, he attended night school, where he studied chemistry, mathematics, law, and Latin. Councill was admitted to the Alabama bar, but he never practiced law in the state. Councill's ambitions extended into politics, and he became the chief enrolling clerk of the Alabama House of Representatives between 1872 and 1874. He also served as secretary of a national civil rights convention in 1873. In 1874 Councill ran unsuccessfully for a legislative seat. One year later, he was offered the federal patronage position as receiver of public lands for northern Alabama. Councill declined the post.

In 1875, the Alabama legislature appointed twenty-six-year-old Councill as the first principal of the State Colored Normal School at Huntsville, which is now known as Alabama A&M University.[66] The school opened on May 1, 1875, with an appropriation of $1,000, in the basement of a Huntsville church. The Colored Normal School would train black teachers to work in Alabama's segregated school system. By the mid-1880s, it rivaled Tuskegee Institute in central Alabama as a vocational-industrial training facility.

Despite his achievements, Councill had his critics. As a contemporary of Booker T. Washington, he and the Tuskegee principal often competed for favors and funds from the Alabama legislature and northern philanthropists. Councill went even further than Washington in his attempt to win the favor of Southern whites by appealing to the upper class's sense of paternalism and racial superiority.

In 1877, Councill founded the *Huntsville Herald*,[67] which he published and edited until 1884. The following year, he established St. John African Methodist Episcopal (AME) Church in Huntsville. Councill worked cooperatively with Elder Bartley Harris and Elder William Gaston and other leading blacks in the community to bring about more involvement for blacks in Huntsville. Councill also wrote several books including,

---

[66] *Southern Advocate*, 1880.
[67] *Southern Advocate*, 1880.

Lamp of Wisdom (1898), *Negro Development in the South* (1901), and *The Bright Side of the Southern Question* (1903).[68]

In 1887, William Hooper Councill attracted wide attention when he filed a lawsuit with the Interstate Commerce Commission (ICC) for being ejected from a first-class coach while traveling on an Alabama railroad. That action later prompted his superiors to relieve him of his duties as president of the state normal school, only to reappoint him in 1888.

The next two decades saw Councill becoming more publicly conciliatory and accommodating toward whites. His stance on race relations was unclear; he regularly praised whites, approved of the "separate but equal" legal principle, and even declared that no people were "better suited for domestic and personal service than the Negro." Despite his earlier lawsuit, he now endorsed segregation, believing it provided opportunities for black businessmen, teachers, and professionals to work among their own people.

In 1884, he married Maria H. Weeden from Huntsville, the first librarian at the normal school. The first high school for blacks in Huntsville was named for him when it opened in 1867.[69] William Hooper Councill High School closed after the schools were integrated in the 1960s.

Maria H. Weeden was Councill's second wife. His first wife died shortly after he became the president of the normal school. Maria Weeden was the daughter of Howard Weeden, who owned slaves during the Civil War. Maria's mother was a slave, and Howard Weeden was her father. Maria was very light skinned and could pass for white, but she was really black—what was known doing that period as mulatto. She did art and other cultural work, but because she was black, she could not contribute her work to herself but, rather, contributed it to her father, Howard Weeden.

While working at the normal school as the first librarian, she met Councill and soon became his wife. Both contributed greatly to the success of the school, as did additional support from her father.

On April 9, 1909, following a long illness, William Hooper Councill died in Huntsville at the age of sixty-one. During the year that Elder Bartley Harris died, Oakwood University was founded in 1896 as Oakwood Industrial School. Legend has it that the school was named for a stand of oak trees found on the campus. It is a private, historically black school

---

[68] *Huntsville Journal*, 1872.
[69] *Huntsville Journal*, 1868.

in Huntsville, Alabama. It is owned and operated by the Seventh-day Adventist Church. The school first opened in 1896 with sixteen students. Classes were offered in various trades and skills.[70]

In 1904, the name was changed to Oakwood Manual Training School, and it was chartered to grant degrees in 1907. In 1917, the school offered its first instruction at the postsecondary level, and in that same year, it changed its name to Oakwood Junior College. In 1944, the name Oakwood College was adopted. The first bachelor's degrees were awarded in 1945.[71]

Oakwood College received its initial accreditation from SACS in 1958, and in 2007, the college received approval to award graduate degrees. In response to this higher accreditation, the school's Board of Trustees and constituents voted to change the name of the institution again to Oakwood University of Seventh-day Adventists.

The St. Bartley Primitive Baptist Church was the leading church at that time, with a great membership increase and an increase of baptisms in Big Spring each month. The rear of the church—located on Oak Avenue, with its gray concrete brick, Gothic windows, and ornamental glass and known as "the Big Brick"—caught fire in1886. And the members held their worship services in the Rust Normal School from 1886 to 1887. The Rust Normal School was a school founded by the Black Methodist church and was said to have been located on Franklin Street.

After the fire on Oak Avenue, St. Bartley was rebuilt with help from white friends, blacks and the United States Government, which sent ($400) to get the building started.[72]

---

[70] Richter-Haaser, "Madison County History," 12–15.
[71] Ibid., 24.
[72] Ibid., 45.

THE CENSUS DATA OF 1860, 1870, 1880, AND 1900

The Madison County, Alabama, census of 1860 as transcribed by Linda Hardiman Smith[73] reflected the names, positions, and ages of the people in Madison County, Alabama. The report showed Elder William Harris, a black male, seventy-eight years of age, a Baptist minister, born 1782 in Virginia, on page 16, section 131/131 of the report. Elder William Harris died in 1872.

Elder Bartley Harris was shown in the 1860 census to be a black male, sixty years of age, a Baptist minister, born in 1800 in Virginia,

The Madison County, Alabama, census of 1870 reflected that Elder Bartley Harris, a black male, seventy years of age and a Baptist minister, was born in 1800 in Virginia. Household members included "Bartley Harris (70), Jennie Harris (wife 64) a female, Minerva Harris (8) female, Lee Scruggs (26), Matt Scruggs (24) female housewife, Frank Scruggs (5) a male, Ellen Scruggs (2) a female, Sam Schaudies (25), male, a shoemaker Abbe Schaudies (21), female, a housewife."

The Madison County Alabama marriage licenses showed that Bartley Harris Sr., married Sylvia Davis on December 26, 1877 (vol. 9, p. 294).

73 Linda Hardiman Smith, "United States Census, 1870,1880, and 1890 for Bartley Harris Sr., Madison County, Alabama."

Bartley Harris Jr. married Rosa Robinson on January 2, 1867, (vol. 5, p. 279).

Bartley Harris Jr., a black male, twenty-four years of age and a farmer, was born in 1846 in Alabama. Household members: "Rosa Robinson Harris, a female, 24 years of age, a housewife, Jennie Spring a female, 13 years of age, a farm laborer."

The Madison County, Alabama, census of 1880 reflected Elder Bartley Harris, a black male, eighty years of age, a Baptist minister, born in 1800 in Virginia. Household members: "Silvia Harris (wife age 65), housewife, Juda Harris, black female, age 70, Lewis Harden, black male age 11, Jessie Buford, black male, age 14.

Bartley Harris Jr., was a black male, age thirty-five, born 1845 in Alabama, was a farmer, residing, Madison, Alabama. Household members: "Rosa Harris, black female, wife (age 35), housewife, Fannie Harris, black female, age 45. Jennie Harris, black female, age 16, John Harris, black male, age 14, Eliza Harris, Black female, age 11."

The Madison County Census, 1900, showed Bartley Harris Jr., black male, age fifty-five, born June 1845, residence, Monrovia, Madison County, farmer. "Household members: Rosa Harris, black female age, 55, Ollie Turner, black male, Lou Turner, Black female, Helena Turner, black female."

The census for 1910 showed Bartley Harris Jr., a black male, age sixty-three, resided in Monrovia, Madison County, Alabama; Rosa Harris, a black female, age sixty-three; Jake Cunningham, a black male, age thirty-two; Maggie Cunningham, a black female, age twenty; Willie S. Cunningham, a black male, age five; Benjamin Cunningham, a black male, age three, and Henry Cunningham, a black male, age two.

Alabama deaths recorded from 1908 to 1974 included Bartley Harris Jr., who died June 6, 1924, in Huntsville, Alabama, age seventy-four. Rosa Harris, his wife, died in 1920 in Madison, Alabama.

THE COURT OF CLAIMS OF THE UNITED STATES, 1901–1906

After the mix-up and distinguishing of the White Primitive Baptist Church and the Colored Primitive Baptist Church, the Court of Claims assigned the White Primitive Baptist Church No. 11,017 Cong. and the Colored Primitive Baptist Church No. 11,690 Cong. The case of Case No. 11,017 Congressional was withdrawn by consent, as there was no claim filed by the White Primitive Baptist Church. During the Court of Claims December term of 1902/03, the record indicated that the trustees of the Primitive Baptist Church, Colored, of Huntsville, Alabama filed a claim for the occupation of and the damage to the building belong to the Primitive Baptist Church, Colored, of Huntsville, Alabama, by the United States Military forces during the late Civil War. The claim was for the amount of $4,000. The claim was not within the jurisdiction of any officer or tribunal of the government, was presented by petition to the Congress of the United States, and a bill was introduced in the United States Senate for the relief of the claimants, which bill, with accompanying papers, was referred to the Honorable Court of Claims for a finding of facts in accordance with the provisions of the act, approved March 3, 1887, and commonly known as the Tucker Act.[74]

Testimonies were taken in Huntsville, Alabama, on June 1, 1903,

---

[74] The Library of Congress, The Tucker Act of March 3, 1887.

from the various trustees of the church. Augustus B. Pryor, a plaster by occupation and seventy years of age, lived in Huntsville, Alabama, during the Civil War and was a member of the church. He testified that the church was on South Madison Street, that he resided a half mile from the church, and that he attended the services held there regularly. He further testified that the church was built by contributions from the slaves around and by what they could beg from their white folks and that it was paid for when it was built. Pryor also testified that "the church was a large frame building and the Yankee soldiers, when they camped here during the war, took it down and carried the material to their camps. It was said that it was used by them in fixing their quarters. The Church was not occupied by Federal soldiers to my knowledge." Pryor testified that "the building was torn down and removed in 1864.[75] One of the buildings was sixty feet, the other was forty feet, with a twelve- or thirteen-foot ceiling. Walls and ceiling were all dressed decorated material for the purpose.

It was weatherboarded with regular weatherboarding, with about one and a half-inch lap. It had a shingle roof; studding was oak and framed into the sills. They were two-by-fours and two feet apart. The joints were two by twelve inches and both were two by ten. They were two feet apart, both below and above. It was floored with regular flooring. The sills were six by six inches and were supported by upright cedar posts, eighteen inches square and three feet long. The brick chimney rested upon the upper joints. The flue was nine by seventeen inches. There were seven windows, each three by seven feet and three doors, three feet ten inches wide and seven feet high. The material was first class and put up with great care. It was built during 1857 and, when taken down, was in good repair, as good as new. The audience room was furnished with beautiful back seats. There were 2 aisles and there were seats on the right and left of the platform on which sat the Minister's desk. It is my recollection there were about 45 or 50 ten-foot seats.

It was a well-built church, and the material was all first class, and I expect that it cost $2000. I never measured the building but know the size it was proposed to be. It stood in the name of the Primitive Hard-shell

---

[75] Testimonies of Trustees of the Primitive Baptist Church of Huntsville, Alabama v. the United States Government, The Library of Congress, The United States Court of Claims (1902–1903).

Baptist Church, Colored. Pryor testified that "the Church was used only for worship of God and was not used or occupied for any other purposes" and that it belonged to the "Primitive Hard-shell Baptist Church, Colored" and "was not sure if it was incorporated in Alabama at that time."

Pryor indicated he was not sure that a body of slaves could incorporate in Alabama at that time. He further stated, "We had a regular minister in charge, colored, and ministers from the white churches visited us often and talked to us and advised us." Upon cross-examination, it was stated that, years before the Civil War, a wealthy old gentleman named Leroy Pope made a present of the land to the colored people, some four acres, for a burying ground and church building, and it had been held by them ever since. It was on this lot that the church was situated and built. A colored man by the name of John Robinson, who was free, and the pastor of the church, who was also free, William Harris, was the leading men in getting up the money to build the church, and William Harris became the church's first founder and pastor in 1820. "No one has ever questioned the ownership of the property."[76]

John Higgins, a farmer who resided in Huntsville, Alabama, during the Civil War, was not a member of the hard-shell Primitive Baptist Church, Colored, but attended the church and was a Baptist. He testified that the church was built in "1856 or 1857 by the members of the church and contributions made by our white folks. Higgins testified that he "lived within five blocks of the Church. The Yankees toted it off on their wagons during the war and took it to their camps nearby to build houses with to sleep in. The church was a one-room building about forty or forty-five feet one way and sixty the other. It had high ceilings, stout studding, and ceiling on the walls and overhead and regular lumber flooring on good stout joists resting on sills. There were four rows of sills. It was weather boarded with a shingle roof. It had beautiful back seats and a brick chimney. The foundation was cedar and all solid wood. It was built in 1856 or 1857 by members of the church and by contributions of the white folks.

Including all who worshipped there, there were over a thousand members. I reckon the cost of the building materials and expenses of putting it up and finishing it was $2100.00 or $2200.00, it would cost $2500.00 to replace it. The Yankee Soldiers took it away and the prized the

---

[76] Ibid.

building apart, as if they wanted to save the lumber from being injured, as if they wanted to use it. A heap of soldiers was there taking it down. Officers were present, hurrying up the soldiers and directing them what to do,"Higgins testified. He emphasized that the building of the church and its business was managed by "Pastor William Harris, and old Uncle John Robinson, free colored men. That the Church was to be paid for by the colored people and their friends." Higgins testified, "The church was not used or occupied by at any time during the war, except for the worship of God."[77]

Testimony was given by Sim Jordan, a farmer, age sixty-five, who lived near Huntsville, Alabama, before and during the Civil War; was a member of the Primitive Baptist Church, Colored, Huntsville, Alabama; and attended services at the church regularly, at least once a week. Jordan testified, "From the beginning of the war until, the building was taken down and removed, it was used only by the members of the Church for church services for the worship of God" He testified, "The building was a large frame building about 40 feet wide, and 50 to 60 feet long. It had a high ceiling and was nicely ceiled both on the sides and was full of comfortable seats. It was torn down and material carried off by the Yankees pulling it down. I saw as many as 50 men taking it down and taking the lumber on their wagons. They said they were going to use the material to make places to stay in. There was a head man who directed them. Their camp was not far off, but I did not go with them but saw how they used it. When the building was taken down it was in good fix, as good as new."

Stafford Pope, a drayman by occupation, age eighty, testified that he lived in Huntsville, Alabama, before and during the Civil War. He testified that he was a member of the church but sometimes could not attend, usually going "once a month."[78] He further testified, "The Church was located in the Southern part of the town, by the graveyard of the colored people, and was built by the colored people. They made money by doing extra work and some of their owners let them raise gardens and chickens and they would sale what they made sometimes to their masters, and we begged money for the Church from the white folks. They would give us money for our church."

---

[77] Ibid.
[78] Ibid.

Pope indicated, as the others had, that "the church was not occupied or used by any sewing society or for any entertainment, fair or headquarters, or sleeping rooms. It was used only for the worship of God."

Pope testified, "The building was erected during the latter part of the Fifties by the members of the church and with what the white folks gave them. It was taken down and carried off by the Federal soldiers when they were camped here during the war that freed us. Cannot give the month or year but it was along during the last years of the war. I know they were Yankee Soldiers. At the time the property was taken, they had camps in every direction and some right up to the town and the loaded wagons went off to the camps. I know there was a big crowd of Yankee Soldiers getting the church. I remember one officer, that was the Wagon Master. He commanded the soldiers that were driving the wagons. The construction of the Church was paid for also by the colored people. They made money by doing extra work. The building was finished inside and had been built some years before the war. It had a wooden roof, but I cannot say whether of boards or shingles. It was called the Hard-shell Baptist Church."[79]

James Clay, a mechanic, age sixty-two, who lived in Huntsville, Alabama, testified that he was an "expert in making up estimates for building contracts and the like." Clay summarized an estimate of the amount and cost of materials and labor necessary to erect the church building: "Materials … \$1457.99; Labor … \$500.00" for a total of \$1987.99."

From the abstracted testimonies of these men, the court noted that the Primitive Baptist Church was a "colored organization composed, in a great measure, at least of slaves."[80]

From the evidence, it was also noted that the church was not used for any purposes during the war other than for those of worship. In view of the facts obtained, the court indicated that the Primitive Baptist Church was "loyal to the Government of the United States and gave no aid or comfort to the Rebellion." The court concluded that the payment to the church would be in the amount of \$1987.99, which was less than the valuation placed on the building by the other witnesses.

In the Court of Claims of the United States, the trustees of the St.

[79] Ibid.
[80] Ibid.

Bartley Primitive Baptist Church filed a brief through the church's attorney Moyers and Consaul and before Attorney General W.W. Scott, Esq., and his assistants, who represented the United States. The trustees as petitioners who represented the church in this case were Stafford Pope, Issac Rice, Allen Boone, Dock Davis, Frank Martin, and Harry W. Laughinghouse (the father of Deacon John W. Laughinghouse Sr., former chairman of Deacon Board).

There were two case numbers involved in the claim—congressional case number 11,017 and congressional case number 11,690.

As case 11,017 moved forward, it was discovered that case 11,017 was subscribed to a White Primitive Baptist Church. The government failed to realize there were two Primitive Baptist churches in the area. One was black and the other was white. No testimony had been taken concerning the White Primitive Baptist Church of Huntsville, Alabama. The findings filed by the court in case number 11,017 were withdrawn by consent, and it was the desire of the Colored Primitive Baptist Church (St. Bartley) to proceed with case number 11,690.[81]

The petition presented by the Trustees of St. Bartley Primitive Baptist Church was that "doing the late war (Civil War) for the suppression of the Rebellion, said church organization was the owner of a certain church building at Huntsville, Alabama; that during said war, the United States Military Forces, by proper authority, took possession of and tore down the church building, belonging, belonging to said church organization and used the material therefore, which, at the time and place of taking, was reasonably worth the sum of nine hundred and nine dollars ($909.00); that during the said war, said church remained loyal to the Government of the United States; that this claim is true and correct that this claim was made subject of Senate Bill Number 3241, 58th Congress, for the relief of said Primitive Baptist Church, Colored, which said bill, was referred to his Honorable court by Resolution of the United States Senate on April 27, 1903."

This was a claim referred to the Court of Claims of the United States under the Tucker Act, and as stated in the trustees' request, the amount was amended for the sum of $1, 987.99, payment for the church being destroyed by the Federal forces during the Civil War.

---

[81] Court of Claims Congressional case No. 11017, September 30, 1906.

A number of witnesses testified, and their evidence was found correctly abstracted in the brief filed herein by the trustees' attorneys. No proof title was offered, except the witnesses testified that the church property was then owned, and still owned, by the Primitive Baptist Church (St. Bartley). The $1,987.99 was found favorable to be amended to that amount by the Court Of Claims and the United States Senate. Abstracts of the testimonies of the St. Bartley trustees are found in copies of the exhibits.

ST. BARTLEY PRIMITIVE BAPTIST CHURCH - 1900-PRESENT

In 1872, Elder Bartley Harris moved the Huntsville African Baptist Church to Oak Avenue, which later became Gallatin Street, on the southwest side of Huntsville. The name was also changed to St. Bartley Primitive Baptist Church. This grey concrete brick building, replete with gothic windows of ornamental glass, was the largest Negro church in Alabama. The church remained on this site for ninety-two years. The last service was a night service, held on the third Sunday in December 1964. Elder Amos Robinson was then the pastor, and Deacon John W. Laughinghouse Sr. was chairman of the Board of Deacons. Deacon John W. Laughinghouse Sr. was the son of Deacon Harry W. Laughinghouse, who served with Elder William Gaston, both of whom served and assisted Pastor Bartley Harris.

Elder William Gaston and Deacon Harry W. Laughinghouse assisted Pastor Bartley Harris with many of the pastoral duties of the church, including the baptizing of new members. With the death of Pastor Bartley Harris on April 2, 1895, Elder Gaston was the associate minister of the church and carried on the services until the church selected Elder Felix Jordan. Deacon Harry W. Laughinghouse served as Chairman of the Board of Deacons and Trustees and worked cooperatively and diligently with Elder Gaston and Elder Felix Jordan.[82]

---

[82] Minutes of St. Bartley Historic Ministry, 68.

THE PASTORS OF ST. BARTLEY PRIMITIVE BAPTIST CHURCH

ELDER FELIX JORDAN

Elder Felix Jordan

Elder Felix Jordan, who was a member of St. Bartley, was elected as the third pastor of St. Bartley and served until approximately the latter part of 1913. Elder Jordan was born March 15, 1864. He died January 11, 1916. He was buried in Glenwood Cemetery. He was pastor at the organizational meeting of the National Primitive Baptist Convention in Huntsville, Alabama, July 17–22, 1907. He attended the national convention also when it was held in Salem, Alabama, in 1913 as pastor of St. Bartley.[83] He was a mover and a motivator, firm and focused. He was seriously involved in progressive thought and firm and focused on his determination to provoke and promote change in north Alabama.

Shortly after his return to Huntsville after attending the National Convention in 1913, he disappeared after leaving the church one night. According to Elders at the time, he was the object of other organizations ill will, but in time his efforts proved to be true.

---

[83] Ibid., 69.

ELDER ELIAS PATTON

Elder Elias Patton

Elder Elias Patton was the fourth pastor of St. Bartley. He too was a member of St. Bartley for thirty-five years before he became the pastor. He served as moderator of the Indian Creek Primitive Baptist Association. He organized and pastored Mt. Zion Primitive Baptist Church for a number of years. It appears that he only pastored St. Bartley for a short period of time.[84]

ELDER RICHARD MOORE

Elder Richard Moore

---

[84] Ibid., 71.

Elder Richard Moore was born to Harriett and Ephrim Moore on Burr Mountain about twenty miles from Huntsville. He also pastored a small church called Blue Spring Chapel located on Blue Spring Road and was a farmer in Harvest, Alabama. Elder Moore became the fifth pastor of St. Bartley Primitive Baptist Church in 1915. He pastored from 1915 until his death in 1950.

Elder Moore was on the trustee board of the William Gaston School and also worked at the Primitive Baptist House. He worked at the Arsenal Signal Corps headquarters at Redstone Arsenal during his pastorship of St. Bartley.

A thrifty man, he put money in war bonds each pay period. During his pastorship, St. Bartley did approximately $7,000 worth of improvements. The church also became debt free during his pastorage.

He was a member of a number of religious and civic organizations, including the Christian Union. He was a most powerful and spiritual minister, as well as a powerful singer of Dr. Watts hymns.

Elder Moore pastored St. Bartley for thirty-five years until his death on April 30, 1950. The church had just celebrated his thirty-fifth anniversary the previous week. St. Bartley then used his anniversary at that time (the fourth Sunday in April) for the April Drive.[85]

Elder Moore's wife at the time of his death was Mrs. Texas Moore. He had a son who is a minister, Elder Richard More Jr. of Lorain, Ohio, and a daughter, Mrs. Annie Robert, of Indiana.

Elder Moore's funeral was held on May 7, 1950, and was officiated by Elder Raymond Gardner of Prospect, Tennessee, and Elder Terry Batts of Mobile, Alabama. He was buried in Glenwood Cemetery on Hall Avenue. Deacon John W. Laughinghouse,Sr., Deacon T. E. Jackson, and Deacon Willie B. Moore, were some of the deacons who served under his pastorship.

---

[85] Ibid., 73–74.

ELDER AMOS ROBINSON

Elder Amos Robinson

Elder Amos Robinson was born in Limestone County, Alabama, to the late Elder and Mrs. Amos Robinson Sr., on April 25, 1912. He was reared in a Christian home at an early age and joined the St. Matthew Primitive Baptist Church and was baptized by the late Elder Ned Patrick. He served as a deacon at that church until he was called into the ministry. He was called to pastor the Mt. Lebanon Primitive Baptist Church in Gurley, Alabama.

In December 1950, while he was working at the Russel Erskine Hotel downtown Huntsville, he heard the voice of God telling him that he would be the next pastor of St. Bartley Primitive Baptist Church. Elder Amos Robinson, in December 1950, was elected the sixth pastor of St. Bartley. Under his leadership, the church experienced great growth. At that time St. Bartley was still located on the historic site on Gallatin Street.[86]

Elder Robinson saw the church, which had stood for more than ninety-two years, be leveled to the ground by the city of Huntsville's wheels of "urban progress." But he and his congregation decided that God could lead them to victory even in what seemed at the time to be defeat. Elder Robinson, along with Deacon John W. Laughinghouse, Sr., and other deacons and trustees (Deacon Perry Watkins, Deacon John W. Laughinghouse, Jr., Deacon D. G. Robinson, Deacon Willie B. Moore, Deacon T. E. Jackson, Deacon Ben E. Wilson, Deacon Lawrence Ward, Deacon. B. Craighead, Deacon Robert

---

[86] Ibid., 78.

Jones, Deacon Rueben Gaines and later, Deacon Levi Freeman) sought property. Along with searching for a new site for the church, the group planned the desired structure and size of the church's new home. Some searched various sites, and others observed various churches.

Once the group visited the University Baptist Church on Jordan Lane, they developed ideas as to what they wanted for the new church. Under Elder Robinson's leadership and among the deacons and trustees, a consensus was reached. Land was purchased on 3020 Belafonte Avenue NW in the Love Subdivision.[87]

Elder Robinson, assisted by the offices and members of the Church, hired a contractor and began the construction of the new church. The structure was designed to accommodate its growing membership. Deacon John W. Laughinghouse Sr., Deacon Perry Watkins and Deacon T. E. Jackson met with the officers at the First Alabama Bank in Huntsville and secured additional funding for the new church.

By this time, there were over four hundred active members, all of whom worked diligently and with great pride to see the fulfillment of their dream of a new edifice. Members were without a real church home for approximately a year while the new structure was being erected. Many of the church activities were conducted in the homes of members. Regular worship services were conducted in the auditorium of the Calvary Hill Elementary School.

Under Elder Robinson's pastorship, more than five hundred members were added to the church. For many years, his ministry extended to vast radio audience of WEUP radio station and through his efforts to win souls to Christ. He would challenge the lost, presenting the plan of salvation and Jesus Christ to them. He visited many garages, barbershops, beauty shops, grocery stores, and anywhere he deemed a place he could present Christ to people.

Many wandering souls were led to Christ. Elder Robinson was a quiet, humble man who would just "be there." Sometimes you would not hear him come into your office or hear him open the church door; he would just be there. If you were not at church or missed church, he would call or come by just to check on you or to see how you were. When he was introduced to you, he wanted to know which was your church home. And if you didn't have one, he wouldn't leave you alone until he convinced you

---

[87] Ibid., 81.

to come to St. Bartley. Every chance he got, he would tell you about the goodness of God and how you needed the Lord in your life.[88]

Elder Robinson was a pastor who was able to forge his membership into strong bonds of love and unity by the force of his great spiritual strength and commitment. It was a happy day when, on the first Sunday in December 1965, he led his flock into the newly constructed church on Belafonte Avenue and listened to them as they raised their voices in praise unto the Lord in the first services to be held in the new church.

The little church on Gallatin Street, starting with the very first national convention in 1907 [and hosting again in 1920, 1939, and 1957], became the convention hosts for the fifth time in 1969, with Elder Amos Robinson as pastor.[89]

The spirit of the founding slaves was evident that first Sunday as the congregation shouted praises unto God and glorified His Holy Name. Elder Amos Robinson, along with Elder Terry Batts and Elder G. W. Gibson, formed a revival team and training that would enhance the growth of the church and the growth of its members.

Elder Robinson was very active in the community. He served as moderator of the Indian Creek Primitive Baptist Association; president of the Tri-State Sunday School and B.T.U. Congress; a member of the financial committee and the board of directors of the National Primitive Baptist Convention, USA, Inc.; a member of the Greater Huntsville Ministerial Alliance; and a member of the Morning Star Lodge No. 50A.[90]

It was at the Huntsville Ministerial Alliance where he met a nineteen-year-old minister, Elder Isaiah Robinson Jr, who was also an educator in the Huntsville School System, and became impressed with his knowledge of the church, and Elder Robinson was to teach a session on Christian Education. After meeting him and persuading him to leave First Missionary Baptist Church, he received the blessings of Dr. H. P. Snodgrass to utilize Elder Isaiah Robinson at St. Bartley.

Elder Amos Robinson became very close to Elder Isaiah Robinson and stayed in constant contact with him day and night. Pastor Amos Robinson wanted to utilize Elder Isaiah Robinson, like Elder Bartley Harris had with

---

[88] Ibid., 102–106.
[89] Ibid., 105.
[90] Ibid., 107.

Elder William Gaston. Pastor Amos Robinson wanted to do something that had never been done in the Primitive Baptist Church. He wanted to make Elder Isaiah Robinson his assistant and for Elder Isaiah Robinson to develop a Christian Education Program at the church, where members would be trained could obtain growth in the Bible. For weeks, he and Elder Isaiah Robinson would travel and visit various homes and areas, contacting members who had been absent and urging others to become members of St. Bartley.

He trained Elder Isaiah Robinson on the procedures and the process of church outreach and other phases involved in the church. Their relationship was like father and son, such a bond of unity and love and respect did they have for each other. He took Elder Isaiah Robinson with him everywhere and to the Indian Creek P. B. Association and introduced him to the brethren. The pair also traveled to other associations and council meetings, where Elder Amos introduced Elder Isaiah to the others. Elder Amos Robinson was the master teacher as pastor teaching his protégée, Elder Isaiah Robinson, the ways and means of the church.

Elder Amos Robinson served faithfully and led his congregation with humility and dedication until the second Sunday in May 1970, when the Lord called him to rest from labor to reward. He worked in the master's vineyard, delivering a soul-stirring sermon at the 11:00 a.m. service at St. Bartley. Then he went to St. Mark Primitive Baptist Church in Athens, Alabama, that Sunday afternoon only a few hours before returning home, where he closed his eyes in blissful sleep. Earlier after the morning worship, he had sent Elder Isaiah Robinson to Shiloh P. B. Church to preach while he went to Athens. After returning home, he called Elder Isaiah Robinson to get a report, which was favorable. The two then talked at length, and Elder Amos Robinson gave Elder Isaiah instructions for what they would do together for the coming week. He finally concluded, saying, "I'll see you in the morning," and noting that he looked forward to the development of the educational program. While in bed at home, Elder Amos Robinson closed his eyes and welcomed the Lord, who took him home to glory.

Elder Amos Robinson's family consisted of his wife, Mother Cleo Robinson; daughter, Annie Bell; and son, Dinsmore.

From May 10, 1970, until October 16, 1972, the church was without an official Pastor.

Elder Isaiah Robinson, Jr., was selected by the officers to serve as interim pastor until a pastor was elected. Elder Isaiah Robinson performed the pastoral duties, preaching as he had been taught by Pastor Amos Robinson—diligently and spiritually.[91]

Other ministers within the Primitive Baptist faith were utilized various time to come and preach during those interim years. Elder R. B. Young, a member of the church also participated.

Elder Amos Robinson's funeral was presided over by Dr. F. L. Livingston, president of the National Primitive Baptist Convention, USA, Inc., and Dr. Terry M. Batts, his close friend and pastor of New Sardis Primitive Baptist Church in Cleveland, Ohio. It was one of the largest funerals and events of that time and attended by thousands. Elder Robinson was buried in Northside Cemetery on Jordan Lane in Huntsville, Alabama.

ELDER V. CASTLE STEWART

Elder v. Castle Stewart

(Photo courtesy of St. Bartley P. B. Church)

During the period of May 10, 1970, through October 16, 1972, the officers saw much in Elder Isaiah Robinson Jr. and his knowledge of Primitive Baptist doctrine and the church. He was very capable of carrying out the duties and responsibilities as pastor, but some of the older members thought he was too young, at the age of twenty, to pastor St. Bartley.[92]

---

[91] Ibid., 116.
[92] Ibid., 120.

So, on October 16, 1972, Reverend V. Castle Stewart became the seventh pastor of St. Bartley and was officially installed in November 1972. Rev. Stewart was called to preach God's Word in 1926 and was ordained in 1932. He had a wide range of experience, with degrees as well as years in the ministry as pastor of various Missionary Baptist churches.

During Rev. Stewart's pastorship, the active membership grew to more than nine hundred members. The total indebtedness of the church was liquidated, and the mortgage was burned on May 13, 1979. Auxiliaries were formed and revitalized, and St. Bartley became more involved in the affairs of the community. The bond issue was met by a renegotiation with Mutual Life and Savings of Decatur, Alabama, and the holders paid.[93]

The church was remodeled, with upgrades to the church inside and out. The basement was dedicated as the Elder Amos Robinson Fellowship Hall. On Sunday, April 22, 1979, the church membership raised more than $18,000 to liquidate the total indebtedness.[94]

Elder Isaiah Robinson, who had served under Elder Amos Robinson, also served under Elder V. Castle Stewart. Elder Stewart saw as much potential in Elder Isaiah Robinson as Elder Amos Robinson did—so much, in fact, that he suggested he attend seminary.

A close friend and the godson of Elder Stewart, Dr. Carl Marbury was an instructor at the Garrett Theological Seminary on the campus of Northwestern University in Evanston, Illinois, just north of Chicago. With Dr. Marbury's assistance and Elder Stewart's persistence, they were able to obtain a full scholarship for Elder Isaiah Robinson to attend Garrett Theological Seminary.

Elder Robinson attended Garrett Seminary as the first Primitive Baptist to enroll there in September 1973, and then, later, Elder J. L. Fitzgerald enrolled. Elder Robinson graduated in June 1975 with a Master's of Divinity from Garrett Theological Seminary.

Due to his declining health, Rev. Stewart's tenure as pastor ended in April 1987. In recognition of his fifteen years of service, he was selected as pastor emeritus of St. Bartley.

Elder Stewart was a native of Camden, Arkansas, and pastored in many states. While pastoring in Arkansas, he married Miss Lurie N. Jackson,

---

[93] Ibid., 129.
[94] Ibid., 142.

and to this union three children were born, Juana Lajoyce, Darryl Sadek, and Nykael Ryad. While Elder Stewart was pastoring in Steubenville, Ohio, nine days before their twentieth anniversary, Sister Lurlie Stewart was called from labor to reward on December 15, 1967.

In 1971, while pastoring the First Baptist Church in Little Rock, Arkansas, he married the former Frances S. Watson, a public schoolteacher in Arkansas for more than twenty-four years.

Elder Stewart's Funeral was presided over by Rev. C. T. Vivian and Dr. Carl Marbury, his godson, along with officers of the Indian Creek Primitive Baptist Association and the National Primitive Baptist Convention, USA, Inc.

Elder Stewart was buried in Menifee Community Cemetery in Menifee, Conway County, Arkansas. During the absence of Elder Isaiah Robinson in seminary, Elder William T. Gladys joined St. Bartley and began to assist Rev. Stewart.

ELDER WILLIAM T. GLADYS

Elder William T. Gladys

(Photo courtesy of St. Bartley P. B. Church)

On April 27, 1987, the church called Elder William T. Gladys as the eighth pastor of St. Bartley Primitive Baptist Church.[95] Elder Gladys, the second child of the late Mr. and Mrs. Thomas Gladys, was born March 5, 1949 in Madison, Alabama. He attended several schools in the Madison County

---

[95] Ibid., 152.

School System and graduated from the Council Training Senior High School. In 1972, Elder Gladys married Ms. Bobbie Toney of Chattanooga, Tennessee.

Elder Gladys accepted God's call to the ministry of the Gospel in December 1979 and delivered his first message in February 1980. He was licensed and ordained by the Indian Creek Primitive Baptist Association in 1981 and 1982, respectively.[96] He was associated with the Mt. Zion Primitive Baptist Church in Madison, Alabama. Elder Gladys served as the associate minister to Elder V. Castle Stewart prior to his election. Under his pastorage, the church experienced steady growth and expansion in its services through many auxiliaries, which served the needs of the members of the church and outreach into the total community.

Elder Gladys held various offices and positions in the Indian Creek Primitive Baptist Association; the Tri-States Primitive Baptist Convention; and the National Primitive Baptist Convention, USA, Inc.

Elder Gladys died on June 3, 2014, at Huntsville Hospital. His funeral was held on June 14, 2014, with Dr. Bernard Yates, president of the National Primitive Baptist Convention, USA, Inc., presiding. Pastor Gladys was buried in Meadowlawn Garden of Peace Cemetery.

Elder Gladys was married to Ms. Bobbie Toney of Chattanooga, Tennessee. They had two children, Nicholas H., and Christopher L.

ELDER JAYMES ROBERT MOONEY AND FAMILY

Elder Jaymes Robert Mooney

---

[96] Minutes of Indian Creek Primitive Baptist Association, 1982.

Elder Jaymes Robert Mooney, a native of Nashville, Tennessee, as of this writing, serves as the ninth senior pastor of the historic St. Bartley Primitive Baptist Church in Huntsville, Alabama. As a pastor and preacher and elder, his passion is to serve God by lovingly leading His people into a deeper relationship with Christ. In March 2017, Elder Mooney became the official ninth pastor of St. Bartley P. B. Church.[97] From 2013 to 2017 Pastor Mooney served as the senior pastor of New Bethel Primitive Baptist Church, which experienced significant growth both spiritually and numerically.

He led the congregation to capital improvements to the church sanctuary and created community-centered projects such as a summer math and literacy program that ministered to more than a hundred students in the Fort Lauderdale community through free tutoring.

Pastor Mooney was active in the Fort Lauderdale community, where he pastored the New Bethel P. B. Church. A lover of learning, Pastor Mooney is a product of the Davidson County School System and Trevecca Nazarene University in Nashville, Tennessee.

In June 2012, he wed the love of his life and high school sweetheart, the former Victoria Cleaves, a graduate of the University of Tennessee-Chattanooga. In February 2016, they welcomed their first daughter, Miss Taylor Noelle Mooney.

Elder Mooney had previously pastored in Tennessee and Florida and was a member of the Cumberland P. B. Association. He had held various positions in Primitive Baptist churches and the National Primitive Baptist Convention, USA, Inc.

In 2019 Elder Mooney led the church in phases of renovations of the church and expansion of ministries. His ministry includes an enriched Christian Education Ministry and a viable Outreach Ministry. May the Lord bless this pastor with the guidance received by former pastors, and may He bless him and his family and keep him to do His Will.

---

[97] Minutes of St. Bartley Historic Ministry, 201.

ST. BARTLEY PRIMITIVE BAPTIST CHURCH, 1862–1964

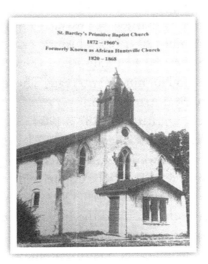

St. Bartley P. B. Church on Oak Avenue
(Huntsville Public Library Special Collections)

St. Bartley P. B. Church on Oak Avenue
(Huntsville Public Library Special Collections)

The St. Bartley Primitive Baptist Church
3020 Belafonte Avenue NW
Huntsville, Alabama 35816

(Photo by Rev. Isaiah Robinson)

In 1970, the Alabama Historic Society, at the request of Elder Isaiah Robinson, the interim pastor at the time, and Deacon John W. Laughinghouse Sr., along with the members of the Board of Deacons and Trustees sought to have St. Bartley be provided a historic marker.[98]

On Sunday, September 20, 1970, a historic marker was placed at the corner of Williams Street and Fountain Row, where St. Bartley Primitive Baptist Church had stood for ninety-two years. The marker was presented by the Alabama Historical Association.

The marker read, "Located here 1872–1964, Saint Bartley Primitive Baptist Church, Oldest Negro Congregation in Alabama. Organized 1820 by William Harris, a slave, who was a minister for more than 50 years."[99] As *The Huntsville Times* reported, "The original church, called Huntsville African Baptist, stood four blocks south in Old Georgia Graveyard. In 1870, this church and three others formed the Indian Creek Primitive Baptist Association. Congregation occupied brick church on this site 1872–1964. In 1965, moved to new building, 3020 Belafonte Avenue. Present name honors Bartley Harris, saintly second minister. Other Pastors: Felix Jordan, Eli Patton, Richard Moore, Amos Robinson. Erected in 150th anniversary year by Huntsville Historical Society-Alabama Historical Association."[100]

St. Bartley Primitive Baptist Church is recognized as the oldest African American congregation in the state of Alabama and is one of the oldest African American congregations in the United States.

---

[98] Ibid., 239.

[99] *The Huntsville Times*, September 20, 1970.

[100] Ibid.

(Photo by Rev. Isaiah Robinson)

The original church structure was built in the Old Georgia Graveyard, which is now the location of the Huntsville Hospital. There is a special memorial to the graveyard and St. Bartley at the hospital.

The St. Bartley P. B. Church Marker Dedication

Present at the unveiling of the marker are Deacon John W. Laughinghouse, Chairman Board of Deacons; Elder W. M. Mastin; and members of the Alabama Historical Association. Present and not pictured were Elder Isaiah Robinson Jr., interim pastor; Elder Eugene Lewis; and Elder R. B. Young.

(Photo by Rev. Isaiah Robinson)

REFLECTIONS

From the Old Georgia Graveyard to 3020 Belafonte Avenue, the St. Bartley Primitive Baptist Church experienced many trials and tribulations. When the church moved to Oak Avenue, the property was donated by Leroy Pope, who owned the property. St. Bartley Church was located in the heart of Huntsville. Many activities drew the attention of large crowds in the surrounding area.

Because the church was so popular and influential, the city of Huntsville and the establishment felt threatened by the power of the many Negroes there at the church, along with its pastors. So lines were drawn to eradicate the power of the church and to maintain white supremacy in the city. For the sake of supposed "urban progress," lines were drawn requiring that St. Bartley be moved in process that became known as "urban renewal." The same tactic was used in many Southern towns to separate blacks from whites. For example, the Southern Railroad tracks would be drawn close to black neighborhoods so that blacks had to "cross the tracks" to get to the town portion of a city while the black community was pushed to isolated areas.

In the modern era, the interstate highways was used to eradicate black businesses. In Huntsville, this affected businesses on Holmes Street, Church Street, and Pulaski Pike and in other areas of black influence. And many blacks who owned property and homes were bought out for little or nothing. Operation PUSH led by Elder Isaiah Robinson and the Huntsville-Madison County Ministerial Alliance led oppositions to the way black was being dis-inherited and phased out of business and homes. The City of Huntsville was put on notice of the concerns of its black citizens and totally ignored the complaints.

From July 17, 1907, through July 21, 1907, a national meeting was called at St. Bartley Church and, for the first time, a National

Association of Colored Primitive Baptist was organized as a conventional body. It is known today as the National Primitive Baptist Convention, USA, Inc.[101]

On May 19, 1908, St. Bartley applied for a certificate of incorporation from the judge of probate, W. T. Lawler. The trustees were Jack McCrosky, Allen Boone, Aik Rice, Frank Mastin, C. H. Ware, Dock Davis (grandfather of Mother Catherine Pendleton), Deacon Harry W. Laughinghouse (father of Deacon John W. Laughinghouse Sr.), and Elder Felix Jordan. On April 9, 1918, St. Bartley Primitive Baptist Church was once again incorporated. The trustees were Tom Coleman, Pearl Macklin, Brewster Townsend, Jeff Moore, and William Hereford.[102]

Saint Bartley was without a pastor from April 1950 to December 1950. During that time, Elder Wesley Alfred Morris was acting pastor. In December 1950, Elder Amos Robinson became the sixth pastor of Saint Bartley Primitive Baptist Church. The last worship service in the "Big Brick" was conducted on the night of the third Sunday in December 1964.[103]

St. Bartley hosted the National Primitive Baptist Convention at its inception in 1907, in 1920, and in 1939 and at the Gallatin Street location in 1969 at 3020 Belafonte. St. Bartley cohosted the national convention with Crumby Bethel Primitive Baptist Church of Birmingham, in Birmingham, Alabama, in August 1983.

St. Bartley's members have always catered to large weddings. An example is the wedding at St. Bartley in1882 of Nanny, a domestic worker, to Jack Turner, a head waiter. For this wedding, engraved invitations were sent out. The church was decorated with flowers and Jackson vine. The ushers wore dress suits, and the bridal party was dressed in light dresses with long trains and carried bouquets of roses. The bride wore a wedding veil of tulle with orange blossoms and a dress with a two-yard train. A section of the church was reserved for white people. It was filled to capacity.

---

[101] Minutes of the National Primitive Baptist Convention USA, July 21, 1907.
[102] Minutes of St. Bartley Historic Ministry, 268.
[103] Ibid., 270.

A more recent example of a large wedding was that of Joyce Robinson, daughter of Deacon and Mother D. G. Robinson, to Edward Ward in June 1983. It was a fairy tale and fantasy wedding just like in the movies with horse drawn carriage, etc.

---

[1] Ibid., 270.

SUMMARY OF CLAIMS AGAINST THE US GOVERNMENT

Historically, the US Claims Court is to pay persons for claims caused by Union soldiers. A. J. Bentley was the administrator of the estate of Elder Bartley Harris Sr. (deceased), in account with Dr. Martha A. Spottswood, in which Bartley Harris was to pay Spottswood one-half of whatever amount was paid by the United States government on a claim against said government, in the name of Bartley Harris for crops destroyed or taken by the Federal Union army in the year 1867 or a few years after the close of the war.[104] The said claim was for $1,020 and was paid in October 1899, one-half being paid to the attorneys for said Bartley Harris and one-half being collected by A. J. Bentley as administrator of Bartley Harris estate in the amount of $510, with $255 going to Martha Spottswood and approved by S. M. Stewart, judge of probate.

Elder Bartley Harris had claims filed against the US Southern Claims Commission for personal losses incurred. Others who filed claims for personal losses were Bartley Harris Jr., and William Gaston. The Bartley Harris era of pastorage was the achievement of many outstanding recognitions for St. Bartley Primitive Baptist Church.

Much progress and recognition were obtained during the Elder Amos Robinson years as pastor. Radio broadcast over WEUP Radio drew the attention of many throughout the Tennessee Valley. Elder Robinson's leadership and sermons were very spiritual and inspirational. He preached no longer than ten to fifteen minutes.

The congregation worshiped and praised God with such fervor that

---

[104] Records of the US Southern Commission Courts of Claims, 1861–1880.

the entire church was completely uplifted. Mother Effie Gaines and the St. Bartley choir's rendition of "Amazing Grace" and her and Deacon Columbus Pendleton's rendition of "When You Hear of My Home Going" *filled* each meeting with the spirit of the Lord or were adored among the congregation or brought the congregation to rapture.

As did Deacon Willie B. Moore's singing of Dr. Watts's hymns. The church rejoiced as they sang and fellowshipped, especially with hymns such as "Father, I stretch My hands to Thee," and, "The Lord My Shepherd Is I Shall Be Well Supplied." The prayer and moaning of Deacon Robert Jones, the melodious singing of Deacon Ruben Gaines, and the shouting of Elder R. B. Young and Elder W. M. Mastin, and the walking of the pews by Elder Isaiah Robinson Jr.—this was score of the golden era of St. Bartley Primitive Baptist church. And it was just as powerfully moving it was under the glory days of Elder Bartley Harris and the large baptisms gatherings.

The next chapters in the life of the St. Bartley Primitive Baptist Church will depend on the unity of fellowship, the love among the sisters and brethren, the praises and true worship of God, the upholding of the principles and doctrine of the church, the teaching of and abiding by the Holy Scriptures, the upholding of the Abstracts of Principles, and the steadfastness of upholding the truth of the Gospel of Jesus Christ. We pray that this body of Christ will continue to allow God to predestine its course of faith and its upholding of God's eternal Word.

FINAL SUMMARY AND REFLECTIONS

St. Bartley Primitive Baptist Church observed its 200th church anniversary in November 2020 (1820–2020). St. Bartley have much to celebrate and commemorate along with blacks in Huntsville who have experienced many things that involved the church since its founding by Elder William Harris in the Georgia Graveyard. After the Union soldiers destroyed the small church building in the graveyard built by the slaves, many incidents happened that have affected the church and the people.

The church relocated to a lot on Oak Street in Huntsville donated by Leroy Pope, on now Williams Street. It was in the heart of Huntsville in a very prestigious and valuable location as Huntsville grew. The slaves doing the census of 1860, 1870, 1880, and 1890 reflected that the black population, including slaves, outnumbered the whites by three to one.

This was a great concern of the white population, and they felt it as a threat. With the leadership of Elder Bartley Harris at St. Bartley Church and Dr. William H. Councill at St. John A. M. E. Church and Rev. Hampton Jones at the Church Street Cumberland Presbyterian Church, valuable leadership was provided to the people of Huntsville. Many blacks occupied leadership and political positions and led in many ways. Among them was Elder William Gaston, an alderman (on city council) for the city. The whites felt that these churches and their leadership were a threat to their manner of life.

In early 1960, the Huntsville City Council, along with enforcing many other discriminatory and racist resolutions and laws, made great use of its power to displace St. Bartley and many black businesses in the city with what became known as "urban renewal"; it should have been called "black removal." Therefore, St. Bartley was displaced from Oak Street to Belafonte Avenue. All the black businesses that occupied downtown Holmes Street, Church Street, and Washington Street, as well as black businesses in the Old Town area were victims of urban renewal.

This was a tactic used to remove blacks and the threat whites felt was a "black takeover." The Southern Railroad was built throughout the south near black communities to separate the white community from the black community, with very little land in the black community for expansion and growth. Blacks had to "cross the tracks" to gain access to downtown and the things offered there, such as grocery stores, drug stores, and other basic necessities.

After the Civil War and Reconstruction, blacks were still mistreated. For four hundred years, blacks have not been afforded full freedom, equal rights, justice, civil rights, economic rights, and other God-given rights and this continues up to the present date. This is why systemic racism became the leading aspect for the white community. Confederate monuments were built to honor Civil War heroes and soldiers. Huntsville, Alabama, was among those cities in the South that made such a move.

The monument in Huntsville, Alabama, was installed in 1905 by the United Daughters of the Confederacy. They had a chapter in Huntsville, where one of the members was Virginia Tunstall Clay-Clopton. In that time, she also led the Equal Rights Association, which was working to get white women the right to vote. In no way was she advocating or working for equal rights among the races. She wanted white women like her to be able to vote and petitioned the 1901 Constitutional Convention for that right. The Huntsville UDC chapter is named for her.

In 1901, Alabama had a Constitutional Convention to amend the state constitution once again. The president of the Alabama Constitutional Convention, John B. Knox, stated in his inaugural address that the intention of the convention was "to establish white supremacy in this State within the limits imposed by the Federal Constitution." Among the many things this convention accomplished, it:

- Outlawed interracial marriage
- Required voters to pass literacy tests in order to register, tests administered by whites to ensure most blacks were rejected

- Ensured a grandfather clause that exempted veterans and their descendants from the literacy tests (because most slaves had been prevented from serving in the military, neither they nor their descendants qualified)
- Required a payment of a poll tax equivalent to almost forty dollars today
- Required racially segregated education

And unfortunately for Ms. Virginia, it still refused all women the right to vote.

On July 23, 1900, Elijah Clark, a black man was lynched outside the local jail downtown. He was tarred, oiled, feathered, and riddled with bullets by a mob of 150 white men, mostly workers from Dallas Mill, after a white woman accused him of assaulting her thirteen-year-old sister. He was lynched after the sheriff had already gotten together a posse to bring him to jail when the mob broke in and took him. He was innocent but was still killed.

On September 7, 1904, Horace Maples, a black man was lynched on the courthouse yard. A mob of two thousand white people came to get him from jail where he was, set the jail on fire, and hanged him from a tree in the courthouse yard.

In 1905, literal steps from where Mr. Maples had just been brutally murdered a few months prior, Huntsville's chapter of the United Daughters of the Confederacy placed a monument of Robert E. Lee outside the courthouse. It read, "In memory of the heroes who fell in defense of the principles which gave birth to the Confederate Cause."

The UDC was part of an effort to repaint the Confederacy and its soldiers as heroes and whitewash history. They erected many of these monuments throughout the South, all explicitly stating that the principles of the "cause" were morally high enough that those who fought could be called heroes.

The monument on the courthouse steps in Huntsville is nothing more than a reminder to the black community that the men inside the courthouse at that time continued to hold white supremacy in regard, and not just among blatant movements or groups like the KKK, but written into the very fabric of law. The courthouse holds the laws and values of the land and populace of which it serves, and those values were wholly for the whites they represented.

It is not a memorial; it is not a noble piece of history. It is a threat, a warning, a finger pointing to the sky that black people did not have equal rights inside that courthouse in Huntsville, and it should be removed from other Southern cities. Finally, in the with the encourage and consideration the monument was moved to Maple Hill Cemetery where it belonged among the dead.

Jim Crow laws and its laws against blacks ensured the injustice continued. Slave patrols formally dissolved after the Civil War ended. But formerly enslaved people saw little relief from racist government policies as they promptly became subject to Black Codes. For the next three years, these new laws specified how, when, and where African Americans could work and how much they would be paid. They also restricted black voting rights, dictated how and where African Americans could travel, and limited where they could live.

The ratification of the 14th Amendment in 1868 quickly made the Black Codes illegal by giving formerly enslaved blacks equal protection of laws through the Constitution. But within two decades, Jim Crow laws aimed at subjugating African Americans and denying their civil rights were enacted across Southern and some Northern states, replacing the Black Codes.

For about eighty years, Jim Crow laws mandated separate public spaces for blacks and whites, such as schools, libraries, water fountains and restaurants—and enforcing them was part of the police force's job. Blacks who broke laws or violated social norms often endured police brutality.

Meanwhile, the authorities didn't punish the perpetrators when African Americans were lynched. Nor did the judicial system hold the police accountable for failing to intervene when black people were being murdered by mobs.

Dr. Martin Luther King Jr. was a lot of things to a lot of different people, but to white America in the time in which he lived, he was absolutely hated. For his work, he was murdered by a white man. The peaceful marches he led often turned violent, as the police let loose attack dogs on the protesters, tear-gassed them, chased them down and beat them, arrested them, sprayed them with the full stinging raw force of the fire hose, and more. There is why the picture we've all seen of the start of Selma's march is called "Bloody Sunday." As a young man at the time, I had the opportunity to participate in the March on Washington in 1963, the Birmingham March, and the Selma to Montgomery march led by Dr. King.

Dr. King believed in peaceful protest, but he also believed in fighting for equality and racial justice through non-violence and knew that would be a hard fight that would not always look pleasing to the white eye. So some of his quotes from his "Letter from Birmingham Jail," as well as some of his other works were inspiring and motivational, encouraging the fight for equal rights for all persons. Dr. Martin Luther King is now historically celebrated part of white America, and I think if that if he would be here today he would wholly and unequivocally condemn what is going on throughout the country.

So now, even in the present twenty-first century, St. Bartley Primitive Baptist Church became the focal point of most of the history surrounding the quest for equal rights and civil rights for the blacks. The leadership of the black slaves and their courage and faith in God provided a platform for the blacks in America to pursue a better day and a better opportunity for all people. The former and present-day peaceful protests reflect the true nature of a people who are tired of four hundred years of mistreatment, killings of black men and women by racist police officers, laws that only benefit the white society, and other discriminatory laws. Change is inevitable. So, the foundation laid by Elder William Harris, Elder Bartley Harris, Elder William Gaston, and other black leaders will not be in vain so long as the black men and women seeks God's guidance, love, and obedience to Him.

I feel that the city of Huntsville, the county of Madison, and the state of Alabama should issue an outstanding apology and resolution to the black community and the St. Bartley Primitive Baptist Church.

The black church has always been the center of hope in the black community and will remain so because Jesus stated, "Upon this rock I will build my church and the gates of hell shall not prevail against it" (Matthew 16:18 NKJ).

The founding of the black church in a graveyard by a slave signified a belief that freedom would come and that slavery would end. Arguably, no episode in US history has left a greater imprint on race relations than slavery. Before the legislation was passed to end slavery, slaves across the world fought for freedom by organizing slave rebellions. In addition, the descendants of slaves fought against attempts to perpetuate racism after slavery during the civil rights movement.

But even once the legislation was passed, it didn't fully mark the end of slavery. In Texas, slaves remained in bondage two years after President Abraham Lincoln signed the Emancipation Proclamation. The holiday Juneteenth was established to celebrate the abolition of slavery in Texas, and it is now considered a day for celebrating the emancipation of all slaves. Racial profiling has become an everyday occurrence, and it impacts more than just the people involved.

An article by CNN uncovered three instances of racial profiling resulting in police being called on unsuspecting black women playing golf too slowly, two Native American students when a mother claimed her children were nervous, and on a black student napping in a dorm at Yale. In the article, Darren Martin, a former Obama White House staffer, said racial profiling is "almost second nature now." Martin recounts when he had a neighbor call the police on him when he was trying to move into his own apartment and how often, when leaving a store, he's asked to show what's in his pockets—something he says is dehumanizing.

Moreover, states such as Arizona have faced criticism and boycotts for attempting to pass anti-immigrant legislation that civil rights activists say has led to racial profiling of Hispanics.

In 2016, *Stanford News* reported that researchers had analyzed data from 4.5 million traffic stops in a hundred North Carolina cities. Their findings showed that police were "more likely to search black and Hispanic motorists, using a lower threshold of suspicion, than when they stop white or Asian drivers." Despite the increased instances of searches, the data also showed that police were less likely to uncover illegal drugs or weapons than with searches of white or Asian drivers.

Religious institutions have not been untouched by racism. Several Christian denominations have apologized for discriminating against people of color by supporting Jim Crow and backing slavery. The United Methodist Church and the Southern Baptist Convention are some of the Christian organizations that have apologized for perpetuating racism in recent years. Many churches have not only apologized for alienating minority groups such as blacks but have also attempted to make their churches more diverse and appoint people of color in key roles. Despite these efforts, churches in the United States remain largely <u>racially segregated</u>.

Churches alone aren't the only entities in question here, with many individuals and business owners using religion as a reason they feel they can deny service to certain groups. A survey by the Public Religion Research Institute found that 10 percent of Americans believe business owners have the right to deny service to black people if it falls under the umbrella of a violation of their religious beliefs. Men were more likely to support this denial of service than women, Catholics were more likely to support it than Protestants, and Hispanics stood as the biggest outlier, agreeing with the right to refuse service to blacks.

Activists, including abolitionists and suffragettes, have long had success in overturning some forms of institutional racism. A number of twenty-first-century social movements, such as Black Lives Matter, and injustice, seek to address institutional racism across the board from the legal system to schools.

REFERENCES AND RESOURCES

Boothe, Charles Octavius, ed. *The Cyclopedia of the Colored Baptist of Alabama, Their Leaders and their Work.* Birmingham: Alabama Publishing company, 1895.

The Library of Congress, *The United States Court of Claims, (1902–1903),* Trustees of the Primitive Baptist Church of Huntsville, Alabama v. The United States Government.

The Library of Congress, The Tucker Act of March 3, 1887.

Oster, Kenneth, ed. *William Harris: The Founder of the African Baptist Church of Huntsville, Alabama., in 1820.* Longmont Church & Society Examiner. Birmingham: Alabama Publishing Company, February 1, 2010.

Crowther, Edward R., ed. *Independent Black Baptist Congregations in Antebellum Alabama.* Washington, DC: Association for the Study of African American Life and History, Inc. 1987.

Owens, Thomas McAdory, ed. *History of Alabama and Dictionary of Alabama Biography.* Vol. IV. Chicago: S.J. Clarke Publishing Company, 1921.

Robey, Diane, Dorothy Scott Johnson, John Rison Jones Jr., and Frances C. Roberts, eds. *Maple Hill Cemetery: Phase One.* Huntsville, AL: Huntsville-Madison County Historical Society, 1995.

Alabama Historical Association. "The LeRoy Pope Mansion, 1814." Historical Marker, 1997.

"LeRoy Pope Obituary," *Southern Advocate.* June 21, 1844.

United States Census, 1860, for William Harris, Madison County, Alabama.

United States Census, 1870 and 1880, for Bartley Harris Sr., Madison County, Alabama

White, Yvonne, ed. "St. Bartley 175 Church Anniversary." *Huntsville Times*. Saturday, September 30, 1995.

Smothers, William, ed. "St. Bartley Church Celebrating 189 Years." *Speaking Out News*. Huntsville, Alabama, September 22, 2011.

Dennis, C. ed. "St. Bartley Primitive Baptist Church." African American History, Huntsville, Alabama, 1808. Blackpast.org. January 31, 2014.

Alabama Historical Association, St. Bartley Primitive Baptist Church Historical Marker Dedication, September 20, 1970.

Price, Elizabeth, ed. "St. Bartley." *Southern Woman's Magazine* (August 1916).

Montgomery, William E., ed. *Under their Own vine and Fig Tree: The African American Church in the South, 1865–1900*. Baton Rouge: Louisiana State University Press, 1993.

Mouser, Kath. *Folklore Family: The Georgia Cemetery*. Huntsville, AL, April 5, 2001.

Harris, Bartley. "The Burning of St. Bartley: An Appeal for Aide." *The Huntsville Journal* II, no. 15. (April 10, 1896).

Fallin, Wilson, Jr. *Uplifting the People: Three Centuries of Black Baptist in Alabama*. Tuscaloosa: University of Alabama Press, 2007.

Baptist, Edward E., ed. *The Half Has Never Been Told: Slavery and the Making of American Capitalism*. New York: Basic Books, 2014.

Kolchin, Peter, ed. *American Slavery: 1619–1877*. 2nd ed. New York: Hill and Wang, 2003.

Sellers, James Benson, ed. *Slavery in Alabama*. Library Alabama Classics. 2nd ed. Tuscaloosa: University of Alabama Press, 1994.

Thornton, J. Mills, ed. *Politics and Power in a Slave Society: Alabama 1800–1860*. Baton Rouge: Louisiana State University Press, 1978.

Williams, Horace Randall, ed. *Weren't No Good Times: Personal Accounts of Slavery in Alabama*. Winston-Salem, NC: John F. Blair, 2004.

Reeves, Robert, ed. *Saint Bartley, the Man and the Church.* WHNT Channel 19 News, Huntsville, AL, February 18, 2016.

Rogers, William Warren, Robert David Ward, Leah Rawis Atkins, and Wayne Flynn, eds. *Alabama: The History of a Deep South State.* Tuscaloosa: University of Alabama Press, 1994.

Fulop, Timothy E. "Primitive Baptists". In Palmer, Colin A. ed., *Encyclopedia of African-American Culture and History.* 4. 2nd ed. Macmillan Reference USA, 2006, 1,836.

Carter, Mo. "Hidden History: Saint Bartley Primitive Baptist Church." RocketCityNow.com. Retrieved November 23, 2019.

Rohr, Nancy M., ed. *Free People of Color in Madison County, Alabama.* Huntsville, Alabama: Huntsville History Coaction, 2015.

Berlin, Ira, ed. *Slaves without Masters: The Free Negro in the Antebellum South.* NY: Random House, 1974.

Cohen, David W., and Jack P. Greene, eds. *Neither Slave nor Free.* Baltimore, MD: John Hopkins, 1972).

Acts of Alabama Assembly, November 1832, 130.

Dorman, Lewy, ed. *The Free Negro in Alabama from 1819 to 1861.* Tuscaloosa, AL: University of Alabama Press, 1916.

Huntsville Southern Advocate. October 15, November 12, and November 19, 1831.

Woodson, Carter G., ed. *Free Negro Heads of Families in the United States in 1830.* Washington, DC: Association of the Study of Negro Life and History, Inc., 1925.

King, Stewart R., ed. *Encyclopedia of Free Blacks and People of Color in the Americas.* An Infobase Learning Company.

Sellers, James Benson, ed. *Slavery in Alabama.* Tuscaloosa: University of Alabama Press, 1950.

Acts of Alabama Assembly, 1820–1824, November 1823, 1878, and 1879, approved 1823.

Robb, Frances Osborne, ed. *Guide to Information on Blacks in Huntsville,*

1805–1820. Dept. of Archives / Special Collections. M. Louis Salmon Library, University of Alabama in Huntsville, Huntsville, A. Series 4, Subseries D.

Betts, E. C., ed. *Early History of Huntsville, Alabama, 1804–1870.* Huntsville, AL: Minuteman Press, 1908.

Huntsville Advocate, February 6, 1878.

Nashville, Republican Banner, January 15, 1860.

Southern Advocate, August 19, 1834, October 7, 1834, and October 1, 1857.

Andrews, Edmund. "Stanford Researchers Develop New Statistical Test that Shows Racial Profiling in Police Traffic Stops." *Stanford News.* June 28, 2016.

Delmont, Matthew. "Why African-American Soldiers Saw World War II as a Two-Front Battle." *Smithsonian*, August 24, 2017.

Greenberg, Daniel. "Increasing Support for Religiously Based Service Refusals."

Maxine Najle, Ph.D., Natalie Jackson, Ph.D., et al., Public Religion Research Institute, June 25, 2019.

Tello, Monique, MD, MPH. "Racism and Discrimination in Health Care: Providers and Patients." Harvard Health Publishing, Harvard Medical School, January 16, 2017.

Ture, Kwame. "Black Power: The Politics of Liberation." Charles V. Hamilton, Paperback, Vintage, November 10, 1992.

Yan, Holly. "This is Why Everyday Racial Profiling Is So Dangerous." CNN, May 11, 2018.

All Scriptures are from the New King James Version of the Holy Bible

Elfriede, Richter-Haaser, "History of Madison County," Madison County Alabama Government, January 2000, 4

Sellers, James Benson. *Slavery in Alabama.* Tuscaloosa: University of Alabama Press,1994, 21.

Kolchin, Peter. *American Slavery: 1619–1877.* New York: Hill and Wang, 2003,19.

Minutes of Meeting of Flint River Primitive Baptist Association, Constitution, 1821.

Minutes of the Indian Creek Primitive Baptist Association, September 17, 1870.

Rogers, William Warren. *Alabama: The History of Deep South State.* Tuscaloosa: The University of Alabama Press, 1994, 110.

1860 Census, Madison County, Alabama, transcribed by Linda Hardiman Smith, June 7, 1860, 16.

Roberts, Frances C., and Sarah Huff Fisk. *Shadows on the Wall: The Life and Works of Howard Weeden.* Northport, AL: Colonial Press, 1962, 8, 9, 12, 13, 15, 19–22, 131. LCCN 63-1883.

Walker, Hugh. "Shadows on the Wall: Howard Who Was a Girl." *Nashville Tennessean* 57, no. 221, December 9, 1962, 13. Gannett Co., Inc. via ProQuest Historical Newspapers.

Pope, Leroy. *Southern Advocate*, Huntsville, June 21, 1844.

Robey, Diane, Dorothy Scott Johnson, John Rison Jones Jr., and Frances C. Roberts. *Maple Hill Cemetery: Phase One.* Huntsville, AL: Huntsville-Madison County Historical Society, 1995.

"Alabama Register of Landmarks and Heritage." Alabama Historical Commission. Archived from the original on January 5, 2008. Retrieved February 13, 2008.

Southern Advocate, 1844.

"

Huntsville Gazette, 1877

Huntsville Journal, 1895

Record, James. *Record II—A Dream Come True: The Story of Madison County and Incidentally of Alabama and the United States.* Vol. II. 1978, 78, 358.

Luttrell, Frank Alex, III, ed. *Historical Markers of Madison County, Alabama.* 2001, 74 and 101.

Pruitt, Raneé G., ed. *Eden of the South: A Chronology of Huntsville, Alabama, 1805–2005.* 2005, 86.

Huntsville Directory Company. "Huntsville City Directory, 1896/97." 93.

Pictures and documents courtesy of St. Bartley Primitive Baptist Church Historical Ministry Minutes, 34–58.

Coolidge, Louis. *Ulysses S. Grant*. Boston & New York: Houghton Mifflin Co., 1917. Scholarly review at doi:10.14296/RiH/2014/2270. Picture courtesy of Mathew B. Brady (c. 1822–January 15, 1896), an American photographer, and one of the earliest in American history.

Calhoun, Charles W. *The Presidency of Ulysses S. Grant*. Lawrence: University Press of Kansas, 2017, 48–56. ISBN 978-0-7006-2484-3.

EXHIBITS

Printed in the United States
by Baker & Taylor Publisher Services